"Creating a New Normal: Cleaning Up a Dysfunctional Life"

By
Sylvia Coleman

Creating a New Normal:
Cleaning Up a Dysfunctional Life
by Sylvia Coleman

Copyright © Sylvia Coleman, 2008
All rights reserved

No part of this publication may be reproduced, stored, or introduced into a retrieval system or transmitted in any form, or by any means, without the prior written permission of both the copyright owner and the above publisher of this book.

ISBN: 978-0-6152-0864-0

Published by:
Write Professional Media, LLC
P.O. Box 2275
Philadelphia, PA 19103
www.writeprofessional.com

Cover design/book layout: Dawn M. Ertel, Accurance,
www.accurance.com
Art /design/web development: Leon Drummond,
www.portfolio.80pproductions.com
Editor: Danielle Campbell-Angah, www.angahcreative.com
Printer: Lulu, www.lulu.com

Publisher's note: Some names and places have been changed to protect the identity of certain individuals.

Acknowledgements:

This book is dedicated to: Mom, Sarah, Michael, the Rochons, Anita, Melinda, Jamal, Andrea, Joanne, Dr. Brown and all those who have contributed to my growth.

I was watching Oprah one day when I first heard the expression, "creating a new normal." The show's guest therapist suggested the phrase to someone who had lost a love one. Although her loved one had been dead for some time, the individual was still mourning her loss as if it were recent, and as a result had stopped enjoying life.

"The normal you once knew with that person is gone," the therapist said. "What you have to do now is create a new normal." I thought about these words a few years after that broadcast when I had lost someone dear to me. Losing him brought up old wounds about my abusive childhood and screwed-up family. After his death, everyone kept asking, "When are you going to get back to normal?" Throughout my own grieving period, I began to reflect more and more on that therapist's advice. It was the only thing that made sense in my terribly depressing world. But how would I create this "new normal?" Who would teach me? And was I really ready to leave my dysfunctional past behind? Oddly, my pain became both a friend and a foe.

I hit rock bottom more than a few times before realizing that the blueprint to my personal happiness was buried beneath all those layers of pain. I share that journey now in hopes that you too can create your own "new normal."

Introduction

Walking up the driveway of the funeral home seemed like an endless path of despair. The knots doubled in my stomach, as I trailed behind Maurice's family through the doorway. I was beginning to feel nauseous. The energy seemed to leak out of my body with every footstep.

Even as I approached the coffin, I did not want to believe it was him. May be there was some mistake. That's right. May be his family had made a mistake, and it was not him lying there. But, even in the dimly lit room, I recognized his form. There he lay, clothed in his favorite suit — a deep navy, business two-piece ensemble that made him look distinctively handsome.

Still, I remained in disbelief, until my eyes found the one recognizable mark that could not deny his identity — a small round birthmark, no bigger than the head of a ball-point pen on his right thumb. I grabbed his hand and gazed at Maurice for what seemed like hours, whispering to him between sobs of snotty tears that now covered my previously stoic face. "I-love-you-baby," I mouthed to his lifeless face.

It was as if a thousand battered souls had climbed into my heart. The love of my life was dead — a 4 ½ -year relationship. Hadn't I already been through enough? It was hard enough for me to trust, let alone love anyone, and the people I did allow myself to trust and love had all died before I reached 30 — snuffed from my life as quickly as they came into it. It's no wonder my first childhood memory is a morbid one.

Chapter 1

Some people claim that they can remember back to when they were babies — usually a first word or some happy experience. Not me. My earliest memory is of death.

I was about four or five years old. My oldest sibling, Lisa, would often babysit me and my older brother, Walter, whom we affectionately called Junyah. What we really meant to say was "Junior," but our Boston accent, notorious for its omission of "r" sounds at the end of words, botched up the pronunciation. I was the youngest, and Junior was the middle child. We both adored Lisa and often battled for her attention.

Lisa was my protector. Living in a three-bedroom apartment, I didn't have my own room, so Lisa and I shared a bedroom, while my brother took the other. From as early as I can remember, I slept tucked beside her, unable to sleep until she slid underneath the comforter beside me. Having her next to me, I didn't mind not having my own bed, and I don't think she minded having me there either. If she did, she didn't complain, and of course I didn't either.

So imagine my disbelief when I woke up one night and she wasn't there! From the bedroom, I could hear coughing in the bathroom. I immediately hopped out of bed and rushed to the bathroom in my

Strawberry Shortcake nightgown. Normally loathing the chill of the wooden floor, I barely noticed the cool draft circling my feet as I sprinted toward the bathroom. I halted at the doorway, stunned by what I saw.

Lisa was leaning over the toilet, coughing up what seemed like an endless stream of blood. I stood in the entrance way, paralyzed. I don't know how long I stayed there, but at some point, my mother, who worked the graveyard shift, came rushing through the door. I still remember the look of desperation on her face. She ordered me back to bed, and I went reluctantly, not wanting to leave my sister's side. I remember thinking, why can't she just take some cough medicine and come back to bed? Lisa had been coughing all week, but I had never seen her cough up blood. My mother rushed her to the hospital at once, and they admitted Lisa overnight.

Meanwhile, my mother dropped my brother and me off at a neighbor's house, an older couple from our congregation. Though it was only for one night, it seemed like we were there for days. I wanted my Mommy; I wanted my bed; and I wanted my Lisa. Finally, my mother arrived. I remember sitting at our neighbor's kitchen table, and, instead of coming straight back to the kitchen, my mother whispered some words to our neighbors in the adjacent room. It was clear she was sobbing, something I never saw my mother do.

Slowly, they made their way back to the kitchen, and although I can't remember her exact words, I recall my mom saying something about Lisa not coming back. I would later find out Lisa had sickle cell anemia, a hereditary blood disorder where misshapen cells get stuck in the blood vessels, blocking blood flow and causing severe pain as well as damage to organs, muscles and bones.

I think I was too young to comprehend the magnitude of that day's events — too young to understand death. Even after my mother took us home, I expected to see Lisa there. I still didn't realize that she was not coming back. I mean, this was my Lisa — the straight-"A," honor-roll student. Back then, those characteristics didn't mean anything to my five-year-old mind. I just knew that when I was hungry, Lisa fixed me a banana sandwich. When I cried after fighting with my brother, she consoled me — snotty nose and all.

Have you ever been around someone whose mere presence made you feel good? Well, that was Lisa. I thought only she and I shared that bond, but as I was soon to find out, many others felt the same way about my big sister. She was exceptionally well-liked and respected in school by both her teachers and classmates. On the day we buried her, I remember seeing rows of people at her funeral, more people than I had ever seen in my life, professing similar feelings for my sister. In fact, she was so well liked by her school that they decided to name an award after her, The Lisa Ann Coleman Award, given to academically exceptional students like herself.

I didn't cry at her funeral; even as my mother's friends and siblings took me in their arms to comfort me, I didn't cry. I didn't grieve about

Sylvia Coleman

her death until many years later. Still, the impact of losing her began to affect me in ways I could not understand.

Chapter 2

My sister's funeral was held in a Kingdom Hall of Jehovah's Witnesses in Boston. Shortly before I was born, in 1975, my mother had converted from being a Baptist to being a member of Jehovah's Witnesses.

Growing up as one of the Jehovah's Witnesses, we believed, as the religion teaches, that our deceased loved ones would be resurrected back to life after God destroyed the wicked and converted the earth to a paradise — a paradise that God promised to the righteous who did His Will. Jehovah's Witnesses consider themselves those righteous, and as God's righteous, they believe they are responsible for spreading the good news about this forthcoming earthly paradise to others on earth. This communication was done through what we called "witnessing," or door-to-door service visits.

This belief was a far stretch from my mother's Baptist upbringing, which preached that the righteous would go to Heaven. According to Jehovah's Witnesses, however, Heaven was reserved for a select few — 144,000 to be exact. These were people like the 12 disciples from the Bible and other early faithful servants of God, like Charles Taze Russell and Joseph Franklin Rutherford, early religious organizers of the Jehovah's Witnesses' faith.

As long as I would get to see my sister again, this seemed like a good belief to me. Having been born and raised a Witness, I had nothing to compare the faith to, nor a need to question the teachings. These teachings brought my mother comfort, too, but did little for my father, who was not a Witness. I'm not sure why he didn't convert, nor did I ever know if he even had any spiritual beliefs or thoughts about life after death.

It was at the Kingdom Hall that I met my good friend, Melody Thomas. She attended the congregation there with her mother, Ernestine, and siblings Paul and Catherine. Melody and I were around the same age and formed an instant bond, just like our mothers did. Melody is the first real friend I recall having. We would spend countless hours playing at each other's homes while our mothers gossiped in the dining room. In time, Ernestine became a second "Mom" to me.

Melody lived in the projects. We would frequently spend the night at each other's homes, but I remember spending most of the sleepovers there at their home, where we would play everything from "Hot Peas & Cold Butter" to "TV Tag" and "Red Light, Green Light." Back then, we spent a lot of time making up games outside. We would play for hours, trying to stay out past sundown.

When I wasn't playing at the Thomas's' house, I hung out with my cousin, Brian, who lived down the street from us on Hiawatha Road. Brian was a peculiar relative. I still remember him coming back from church, jumping out of the car, still stomping his feet, clapping his hands, and belting out the latest hymn from Sunday's church service — all in the middle of the street! Brian was the youngest of seven siblings and had lots of toys. Although his mom would buy him the latest toys, his favorite was Barbie. I don't know if anyone else in the neighborhood knew it, but Brian not only had all of the current Barbie dolls; he also had the Barbie Dream House!

Although Brian relished his Barbie empire, he had another favorite — Wonder Woman. Back then, Wonder Woman was one of the most widely-watched "super hero" programs on TV. Everyone admired her and her fantastic feats, including my cousin. In fact, Brian loved her so much that he would often sprint around the house draped in a "cape" singing the "Wonder Woman" theme song in his pajamas. Boy, what a sight! We teased him relentlessly about his girly toys, mostly out of jealousy because our parents couldn't afford such wonderful gifts. Besides, Brian received most of his toys for birthdays and holidays, neither of which we celebrated as Jehovah's Witnesses, since it was against our religion. I recall ignorantly speculating that Brian was gay, but as we got older, he grew out of his dolls and more into girls.

As a young child, holidays were especially hard — not so much around family, but during school when all the teachers led the children in making holiday gifts or hosted holiday parties. I had to leave the room and sit in the library on those occasions. I would try to sneak out of the classroom quietly, so no one would see me. Occasionally though, I would catch the wandering eye of a classmate or two who would look at me with pity — a look I would continue to see from my peers throughout my school years. I guess some of my teachers felt the same way because they always tried to save me something from their holiday parties.

Indeed, this was just the beginning of my religious upbringing and conspicuous separation from non-Witnesses. As I grew older, I was also restricted from parties, dances and other social gatherings that involved people outside of the religion. At times, being one of the Jehovah's Witnesses was alienating. However, as alienating as it could be, I don't regret my upbringing as a Witness. It instilled priceless values and ethics in me that helped me avoid many pitfalls during later difficult times in my life.

Chapter 3

Ironically my mother and father, both from Alabama, did not meet until they moved up North, where my father became a truck driver for a Boston-based chicken company. As a child, I remember eating a plethora of chicken, so much in fact that I became addicted to the stuff. I would later find out that my father was stealing these chickens from his job. My father also loved fishing. So, when we weren't eating chicken, we were chomping down fried catfish.

Two of my fondest memories with my Dad are related to meals. I recall a diner my father would take me to every morning before pre-school as a toddler. The diner, nothing but a mere "hole in the wall," was directly in front of my bus stop. My Dad would treat me to toast and eggs. I'd sit at the table swinging my legs up and down, enamored not only by each bite of my yummy breakfast, but also by the chocolate man smiling across from me. I felt the closest to my father during those early morning getaways. Caught up in these moments, there were times when we had to dash outside so I could catch the bus on time. Still, it didn't matter how tardy we were, my Daddy never forgot to give me a proper send-off. "Give me some shugga," he'd say. I'd hoist myself up on the tips of my toes, feeling the bristle of his mustache as I leaned in for our departing kiss.

Meals were a center of social interaction in my family, so it is no wonder the other biggest memory of Dad centered on food. My father was a take-out kind of guy, and my siblings and I took full advantage of this weakness to score fast food — and time with him. We lived in Mattapan, Massachusetts, so the closest place to get burgers and fries was the Burger King in Mattapan Square. If Dad was going to take us to Franklin Park and hang with his buddies there, we knew we could convince him to buy us some Burger King along the way. I think Dad was all too happy to do this, so he could keep us occupied while he drank beer with his park buddies.

Back then, the Burger King kid's meal came with a king's crown. It didn't matter how many times we went to Burger King; we had to get crowns! In fact, I think we loved the crowns more than the other toys that came with those meals. Once we gobbled down our burgers and fries, the trip was on to Franklin Park. If my mother had known we were running wild all over that big park out of Dad's sight, she would have had a fit! Happy memories of time with my father lessened after my sister died. I can't remember how he dealt with the loss of my sister, but I can tell you that my sister's death was the beginning of the end of his relationship with my mom. You see, my mother blamed my father for what happened to my sister.

During this time, my mother worked two jobs and was unable to take time off for a doctor's visit, so she had to depend on my dad to take care of us kids. In the days that preceded Lisa's death, my mother repeatedly asked my father to take Lisa to the doctor. According to Mom, he kept putting it off, convinced it was not that serious. But Lisa's coughing got progressively worse — so much so that my mother had to keep her home from school. When my sister died, Mom's animosity toward Dad grew. I think she bottled up most of her feelings inside because I don't recall her openly dealing with the grief. I think she was overwhelmed with the emotions, because she certainly didn't notice the way her two remaining children were now falling apart.

Chapter 4

Things in my family were never the same after Lisa passed away. My mother packed up my sister's belongings — pictures and all — and to this day, I don't know where she sent them. It would be years before we would speak of Lisa again, and beyond her funeral day, we never went back to her grave.

However, I do remember one occasion of comfort, when I climbed into bed with Mom and Dad and slept, tucked between them in silence. Eventually, I had to return to my own bed. With my sister no longer there, I hated sleeping alone, so it was decided my brother would keep me company at night. Although this decision was initially comforting, it didn't take long for things to fall apart. My brother, Junior, was a problem child for as far back as I can remember. Even as a baby, my mother said he'd wail all through the night with a relentless cry. It was as if nothing or no one could comfort him. Like any parent, Mom hoped he would grow out of it. To the contrary, the older he got, the more unmanageable he became.

After my sister died, his behavior got worse. In fact, it became downright bizarre. Whenever my mother turned her back, he started pulling down his pants and flashing his genitals at me. Apparently flashing wasn't enough, so he escalated to rubbing and pulling his genitals. He seemed to like the secrecy and thrill of doing it, especially when my mother went into another room. His face would light up with sheer excitement, and he'd smile and giggle at his defiance. To him, it was a game. And, like any game, it needed to be shared, so he coaxed me into "playing" too. Before I knew it, we were flashing each other. Too young and ignorant to understand the true nature of this "game," I continued to play at his insistence. Still, something felt shameful about this act. And anytime I was reluctant to play, my brother insisted it was a "normal" game that everyone played.

I guess the thrill of the act begin to wane for him, because he moved on to a new "game," one that involved touching. He called this game "humping." One night, he described this "game" and how much fun it would be. He then pulled down his pants, exposed his genitals, lifted my Strawberry Shortcake nightgown, and began thrusting his pelvis up and down over mine. Looking back, I don't think he knew exactly where to put his penis, but it didn't stop him from trying. This "game" didn't feel like fun, but he assured me and my five-year-old mind that it was "normal." Pretty soon, I began to loathe bedtime, not knowing what he would try next. But I was too afraid to tell anyone I didn't like his "game." After all, he had said it was "normal." He was my brother, so I didn't think he would intentionally hurt me.

Perhaps even worse, his behavior started to rub off on me. Junior continued to reassure me that flashing and humping was "normal," so when I played with Barbie and Ken, I began making them hump each other. I also flashed a friend of mine and tried to convince him that it would be fun to flash me back. Thank God that friend had the sense to refuse. I never tried to flash any of my friends again. I shudder to think that had this friend reciprocated my actions, I could have become a perpetrator too and continued my brother's sick game with other children. I wasn't proud of this behavior. In fact, at that time, I wasn't sure why I did it. But I can tell you that I suppressed these memories for many years, not realizing that what had happened was sexual abuse.

Around this time, I became more withdrawn physically and emotionally. Everyone just thought I had an ingrained "attitude problem." It became difficult to make and keep friends. Inevitably, I would find a reason to kick them out of my life. This behavior, unfortunately, became a lifelong habit with everyone who attempted to get close to me. The only person I wanted to hang around was my good friend, Melody. Physically, I couldn't stand to be touched by anyone, not even my Mom; I would not allow her to bathe or hug me. Growing up, my brother and I frequently fought and argued. In fact, I detested being in the same room with him, especially after the last abusive incident.

I can't tell you how long the abuse went on, but I can tell you when it ended. My brother decided to take the "game" to his room while my mother was in the kitchen cooking. My mother came into the room to check on us. Junior quickly scurried under a pile of laundry on his bed in an attempt to cover his bare body, as I tried to pull my nightgown over the panties that hung suspended around my thighs. My mother had the most rageful look I had ever seen on her face. That day, she didn't wait for my father to come home from work with his belt. She wailed on me and my brother until the energy drained from her hands and she could no longer spank us. It's difficult to describe how shameful, dirty and confused I felt at that moment, not understanding why this "game" had provoked such an intense outburst from my mother.

Although that was the last time my brother forced me to play any of his games, that was not the end of the abuse. My brother found a new victim. Her name was Janie. She was spending the summer with her grandmother, who lived next door. Janie was a fair-skinned girl around my brother's age. She and my brother teased each other relentlessly.

By this time, my brother and I were staying home by ourselves. He was in charge of watching me while our parents worked during the day. My mother gave us specific orders never to have company over (including our cousin, Brian) when she was not at home. Anyone who knew my mother knew "she was no joke" — she said what she meant and meant what she said. But my hardheaded brother always found a way to slip someone into the house while my mother was at work. Usually, it was my cousin, Brian, but it wasn't long before he tried sneaking our new neighbor, Janie in as well.

It took a bit of coercing to get Janie in the house, but once he got her there, Junior forced her into the bedroom. I tried to shove my way in, but I was no match against the strength and size of my older, stout brother. He was easily able to lock me out. Janie beckoned Junior to let her go. Like an amplified echo, I could hear hitting, slapping and objects shattering in the room. I pounded my fists and jerked my feet against the door, pleading to get inside.

The minutes the two were inside that room seemed like hours. I can't say I know for sure what happened in there with Junior, but I've often wondered if he did to her what he did to me. After some time, Janie managed to break free. The door flew open with such force that it ricocheted off the wall. Janie bolted out, struggling to stand. Her hair was tousled in all directions across her scalp. Panting for air, Janie's now scarlet face was soiled with tears. "I'm-going-to-tell-my grandmother!" she howled back into the room. My brother tried unsuccessfully to get her to calm down. She scuttled out of the house like a rodent scampering from a starved alley cat, and Junior could not stop her. All he could do was wait until my mother got home. Scared of what she would do to him, the wait seemed like an eternity.

Janie's grandmother was livid. She told Mom what had happened and banned Janie from visiting us. My mother came back into our house like a pit bull ready to attack. When my mother got mad, she pursed her lips together and talked through clinched teeth. Looking back, I don't know which "whupping" was worse — the one he got when she discovered him naked under the laundry or this one.

Chapter 5

There was never a dull moment living on Hiawatha Road in Mattapan. You would think my brother would have learned his lesson about letting people in the house after that incident with Janie. Not!

He paraded all kinds of kids from around the neighborhood in and out of the house. Always attracted to the worst people, my brother let a group of shady boys from down the street into the house one day. Now granted, we weren't a wealthy family; in fact, we were barely middle class, so we didn't have much. Still, that didn't stop my brother from exhibiting what little we had to a skinny kid named Trey and his crew. My brother gave them a tour of everything, from my mother's big, glass Snoopy bank of pennies to the jewelry box she kept concealed in her closet. Can you say, "Stupid?"

Meanwhile, my mother decided to put us in Lena Park Day Camp to keep us occupied and to avoid a repeat of the last summer's fiasco with Janie. My brother and I loathed this camp. The counselors were older teenagers that barely paid us any attention. Plus, with the exception of swimming, art class and a playground, the camp's activities were scarce. Still, I continued to go, because my best friend at the time, Stacey Brown, was going too.

Once Trey realized we had gone off to camp, he began plotting his break-in. It didn't take long for him to strike. Days later, we came home to a busted window. It wasn't evident at first that anything was missing, but, my mother started taking inventory of our possessions. She noticed her penny jar was gone, as well as a small, black velvet pouch from her jewelry box. It seemed like the "devil" jumped into my mother when she realized that pouch was missing! Examining the clues, she took note that nothing else in the house was taken or in disarray and surmised the thieves knew exactly what they were looking for before they entered the house.

Her conclusion was that it was an inside job. She wanted to know who we invited into the house in the days that preceded camp. She interrogated me and my brother over and over until he finally confessed to showing Trey and his friends around the house. Before I could bat an eye, she yanked up my brother and marched him down to Trey's house to confront him and his parents. She instructed me to stay home. I peered out the window, anxiously waiting for them to return. I have to admit, I was scared. Even though I wasn't the one in trouble, I was nervous about what my mother would do. It seemed like they were down the street forever, because when they left, it was light outside. As it started to get dark, I became increasingly worried. I thought about going there, but didn't want to risk receiving any of my mother's fury.

It was a good thing that I didn't leave the house, because no sooner had the thought entered my head, their silhouettes emerged onto the street. What I saw next was incredulous. My mother was whupping Junior all up the street! Apparently, after she got her velvet pouch back from Trey, she began spanking my brother right in front of his friends! You see, my mother is a Southern woman with old school values. She didn't care who saw her hitting my brother, and she sure as hell didn't care if my brother was embarrassed. Still, I wondered what was so special about some pennies and a little black pouch. Later that evening, when my mother began to calm down, I found out.

"The pennies, I don't care about," she said, "but that pouch had some rare coins from the 1800s and a locket with Lisa's picture on it … the only picture I have left of her."

Finally I understood. Up until this point, I thought my mother had discarded all the belongings, memories and pictures of my big sister. I didn't know she had kept one remaining photo, no bigger than a dime, in that little black velvet pouch. In that instant, the shame and embarrassment of that day's situation dissipated. I didn't care what the kids on the street would say tomorrow about my mother spanking her son all the way up Hiawatha Road. I felt sorry for my mother and realized that her anger had not been anger at all. It had been sadness and pain. Like each one of us, she too had a need to hold on to a piece of Lisa

Chapter 6

As you can see, there were definitely some rough times on Hiawatha Road, but there were also some pleasurable ones too. Like when I first got my cat, Spot. I'll never forget that day. My cousin Brian's cat had just given birth to a litter of kittens, and we were invited to take one home. My mother took me over to Brian's house to pick out a kitten. All were some variation of black, white and gray. They huddled around each other, creating a big circular mass on my cousin's porch.

Watching the kittens play together was as much fun as trying to pick one out. True to form, I couldn't decide which one I wanted. "Hurry up and pick one out so we can go," Mom teased. She wanted to get home and start dinner. Quietly, I pointed to a kitten scurrying among his siblings. He had a black/grayish spot on the middle of his forehead. I patted my mom to draw attention to him before he got away.

"That one, Mommy! That one!" I squealed.

My mother reached down and picked up the wrong cat. I guess it was hard for her to hear me amidst all of the meowing.

"No, that one!" I said, pointing to the one with the spot.

"What's the difference?" she asked. "They all look the same. Why do you want that one?"

"Because he said, 'New York,' Mommy."

"What?!"

"Listen," I said. To my six-year-old mind, the cat's meow sounded like he was saying "New York." She leaned in to listen and started laughing, finally understanding what I imagined I'd heard. My mother still kids me about that incident as if it happened yesterday. "What are you going to name him?" she asked.

"Spot," I replied, as if I was stating the obvious.

"Spot? Why Spot?"

"Because he has a cute little spot on his forehead."

We got Spot home, and he became a part of the family. Until then, I don't think anyone in my house had ever had a pet, because Spot never did quite get housebroken. Besides a litter box and some food and water, we never bought anything else for Spot, like a scratching post. So Spot constantly clawed up our sofa. The seats of this particular sofa were made with gaps between each cushion, so Spot would sneak up under the sofa and scratch you with his sharp nails. It was uncomfortable to say the least, but it still wasn't as bad as forgetting to get Spot a flea collar which, unfortunately, we did.

Soon, we began to itch from the fleas — there were lots of them. In fact, I still itch when I think about it. Fleas were everywhere — in the bed, in our clothes and on Spot's favorite "scratching post," our couch. Who knew one kitty could attract so many fleas? I can't remember how we got rid of them, but I do know that we started putting Spot outside on the porch. One day we came home and Spot was no longer there. Evidently, the kitty had run away. I was devastated! Every time we hopped in Mom's car, I hung out the window, peering about for Spot. Poor Spot, I thought. He's all alone. After a couple of weeks, we gave up. I never saw Spot again. He was our first and only pet.

****

Thank God, I still had my cousin, Brian, whom we played with practically every day. We played "Hot Peas & Cold Butter" or "TV Tag" almost daily. Then, for some reason, I decided to play something different one day. Back then, a lot of kids had Easy Bake ovens. I didn't have one, so I decided to make mud pies from dirt in a nearby empty lot. Big mistake! No, a huge mistake!

My mother had warned me many times not to put my hands in my mouth when I came in from outside unless I washed them first. Back then, I was a hard-core thumb sucker. In fact, my good friend, Melody, and I were finger-sucking addicts — she sucked her two middle fingers. After I finished my brown, gooey mud pies, I shoved my thumb right into my mouth.

A few days later, I started itching. Not all over like when we were exposed to the fleas, just in my underwear. Initially, I was reluctant to tell anyone because I was too embarrassed. Besides, I knew that telling would mean I would have to be examined, and I couldn't stand being touched especially in such a private area of my body. I assumed a good bath would rid me of my itching. Normally, my mother had to fight me to take a bath, but this time I went willingly — and even ran my own bath water. Unfortunately, the bath didn't help; the itching continued. Later on that evening, I went to the bathroom before climbing into bed, only to discover tiny white worms in my underpants! I cupped my hands over my mouth to suppress a scream.

Although horrified and embarrassed, I had no choice but to tell my mom if I wanted to be worm-free. She immediately checked me out and took me to the doctor the next day, where I received some ointment and oral medicine. The doctor confirmed that it was probably from sticking my thumb into my mouth after making those mud pies. Eventually the worms went away, but we had to discard all the towels and washcloths I used during the time I was infected. That was a small price to pay to get rid of those icky worms. I never sucked my thumb again, but I didn't stop playing in the dirt. I was just more cautious about washing my hands afterwards.

****

As I said earlier, there was never a dull moment on Hiawatha Road. As strange as my cousin Brian was, he could not compare to his bizarre neighbor, a man named Richie who lived with his parents.

Brian's parents had rented the upstairs apartment to them in the three-family house they owned. Richie was nicknamed "Crazy Richie" by us kids. My mother always said that the way he behaved, he was possessed by demons.

Some may find his behavior incredulous, but we saw Richie do unfathomable things. Like the time me, my brother and some neighborhood kids saw him running down the street alongside a car going over the speed limit. Richie also had unpredictable fits of anger. My cousin Brian swore he could hear Richie's father beating him with something heavy in the middle of the night. I don't know how true that story was, but I do remember the time I was playing on the porch with a neighbor and Richie took one of his fits of anger out on me and my playmate.

My brother and cousin had a nasty habit of teasing Richie. Too young and ignorant to understand the consequences of their actions, they harassed him out of boredom I guess. Big mistake! Seeing how angry he was one day, they took off running. And before my friend and I could blink, Richie was headed in our direction. Not knowing what he would do, we tried to run into my friend's house, but the front door was locked, and we could not get inside.

To this day, I am still awestruck by what happened next. In his fury, Richie picked up a huge rock. Not just any rock, but the type of boulder-sized stone a construction excavator would have to lift. This was it! Our young lives would soon be over. My friend and I locked arms, clutched each other tight in a corner of the porch, and cried like babies. We just knew he was going to hurl that boulder at us.

Fortunately for us, he didn't. Richie chucked the huge mass into the gravel a few feet away from the porch and stormed back across the street, disappearing into his apartment. Whew! What a relief! Some didn't believe our story, and looking back, I can't really blame them. I mean, we were just a couple of seven-year-olds. But my friend and I knew the truth. You never forget something like that. Besides, even the naysayers could not explain how that big rock got from one side of Hiawatha Road to the other.

Chapter 7

While my brother was acting out at school, I had taken on a new role in the family as the "model" daughter — a desperate attempt to fill my sister's empty shoes in the household. I didn't realize what I was trying to do at the time. I wouldn't figure this out until years later, and it would take even longer for me to realize that there was only one Lisa, and she could never be replaced.

Even though my brother and I fought bitterly, I tried to excel in other ways to retain some kind of normalcy in the house: I cleaned my room, behaved in school, sat still in the Kingdom Hall, and took a bath every night. Little did I know I was becoming a perfectionist. My passive attempts to keep the family normal were just that, passive and unnoticed.

In the weeks and months that followed Lisa's death, my mother and father grew further apart. My mother could no longer share her life with a man she blamed for her daughter's death, so she packed up my brother and me, and we left for another part of Mattapan — Lorna Road.

Mattapan, nicknamed "Murderpan" because of its high murder rate, was a part of a cluster of Boston subdivisions that were considered the "badlands." The main other areas were: Roxbury,

Dorchester, Jamaica Plain, Mission Hill and Hyde Park. I was both sad and elated about the move. I didn't understand why we were leaving Daddy and my cousins, but I was happy we were moving closer to my good friend, Melody, who lived right up the street in the projects.

By this time, I was a latchkey kid and as self-sufficient as any seven-year-old could be. I was often home alone while my mother was at work and my brother loitered on the streets. But being self-sufficient didn't prepare me for what happened one day when I was home by myself.

That day, I wasn't feeling well, so my mother let me stay home from school by myself. She gave me explicit instructions not to answer the door and also showed me how to prepare my lunch. After she left, I hopped into bed to watch cartoons.

To my dismay, there weren't many on, but I watched TV anyway. Eventually, I drifted off to sleep, only to be startled by a thunderous crash at the back door. I tiptoed into the kitchen and pressed my ear against the rear door of our apartment. There was some sort of banging and scraping going on. Then, boom! The door slammed onto the floor. Not my door, but the second door, which led out to the back porch. I jumped, quickly covered my mouth to quell a scream and slowly retreated from the door.

For a few seconds, the noise stopped. Then I saw the door knob turn. The banging resumed. Someone was thrusting their body against our door. I couldn't believe it. Someone was trying to break in! Terrified, I sprinted to the front of the apartment, frantically looking for a place to hide. As I raced about, the pounding ceased. Whew, I thought. They gave up. Not! Now I could hear drilling. Persistent, the intruders were using a power drill to unhinge the door. There was no time to wait; I had to act fast.

I figured it was a matter of minutes before they busted into the apartment. With few options for hiding, I slid underneath my mother's queen-size bed, praying they wouldn't find me there. Tears and snot were coming down faster than I could wipe them away. I was too scared to go to the bathroom to get tissue, so I wiped my face and nose with the ends of my nightgown. I wanted to call Mom at work, but I was afraid the burglars would hear me. The minutes seemed like hours. Unable to get the door open, they left and made their way upstairs to our landlord's apartment where the drilling resumed. It took them no time to unhinge their door. Still, I remained trembling underneath the bed, not knowing if they would come back down to our apartment.

I could hear objects smashing and dropping in each room upstairs for what seemed like hours. Finally, their footsteps resurfaced on the stairs, and they raced out the door. Still, I didn't dare move. I don't know if I was in shock or just terrified they would come back; I was probably feeling a bit of both emotions. After a good half an hour, I emerged from under the bed, peering around corners before making my way to the phone to call my mother, who immediately phoned the cops. The police came to inspect the apartments and concluded the only reason our apartment was spared was because our door hinges were blocked by the adjacent basement door. To unhinge our door, the robbers would have had to remove the basement door first. Call them dumb thieves if you'd like, but I know now that I was spared by the Grace of God that day.

****

Some might say the same of my brother, too. As I mentioned earlier, Junior was a magnet for trouble. He didn't have any problem seeking out the wrong crowd in our new neighborhood.

He met a kid up the street who was around the same age and like him was always getting into or starting trouble. Junior had his share of run-ins with this kid, and my mother urged him to keep his distance. "Stay clear of that one," she advised. And it was a good thing she did. Shortly after that conversation, the boy was found in the woods down the street, gutted by a sword.

After that, I thought things couldn't get worse, but I was wrong. Next door to us, there lived a couple with a son. We used to laugh at the husband all the time because every Sunday, he would meticulously wash and wipe down his car, inside and out. He was "pimping out his ride" before the MTV show! I can't say I ever saw him miss this weekly ritual. My family and I couldn't help but snicker at our car-obsessed neighbor. It was one of those odd things that can make urban living so fascinating — everyone was strangely original.

So imagine our surprise when we didn't see our neighbor outside attending to his car for a couple of weeks in a row! We joked that maybe he'd found a new hobby. Life went on until one day we came home and saw yellow crime tape around his house. Everyone was whispering that someone was dead. Who? Not someone next door to us! We turned on the news, and behold, there was footage of our neighbor's son being taken from the house in handcuffs. Apparently, the police entered their home while we were gone during the day. The wife discovered her husband's body in the attic when she went up there to retrieve some clothing. The son had shot his father and hid him in a corner of the attic.

We were astonished. It was unbelievable that someone living next door to us could be murdered. That tragedy was all we could talk about for days. After that, we never saw the mother or the son again. As much as we mocked the way our neighbor obsessed over his car every week, we couldn't help but miss him. Seeing him out there, added to the character of our quirky neighborhood.

Chapter 8

As drama-filled as Boston was, there was something I always deeply loved about living in the city. I have fond memories of going to the annual Boston Kite Festival and the Caribbean Festival, two of the city's biggest events held in Franklin Park along Blue Hill Avenue, one of the city's main streets. These two events are still held today and are all about the music, food, fashion and entertainment.

One of my favorite memories of the Kite Festival was when the R&B group, New Edition, performed there in the mid-1980s. Back then, New Edition was the most recognized band to come out of Boston. Our local black radio station, WILD, played the group's music nonstop, so everyone was really hyped that they were returning to town to give a free mini-concert at the festival. I was excited too and hoped they would sing my favorite songs: "Candy Girl," "Mr. Telephone Man" and "Is This the End." But unfortunately, like previous kite festivals, the concert was interrupted by violence. My mother quickly took us kids away before the end of the show.

By this time, I was eight — old enough to take the bus to school by myself. I was attending a new school, the William H. Ohrenberger Elementary School, in Hyde Park. Ohrenberger was my favorite school by far. I loved everything about it — recess, the classrooms, even the library. Ohrenberger prided itself on cultural diversity, and included special classrooms for children of Laotian refugees and a yearly International Food Day for students, parents and teachers.

I was a budding entrepreneur back then and gained attention by drawing Cabbage Patch Kids and selling them for a quarter to my classmates. I used the money to buy my lunches. My mother had signed me up for the free lunch program, but I didn't want to get free lunches because I didn't want my classmates to know how poor I really was. Other kids who weren't well off got teased, and I didn't want to be one of them.

But how much money your family had wasn't the only criteria that made you a target for ridicule at my new school. I remember how everyone picked on a girl named Shanika Moody. Shanika was an average-looking girl, neither ugly nor pretty, but she was skinny and had a long nose and lanky body. No one liked her and they went out of their way to show it every chance they got. She was a prime example of what happened to those who were teased.

Kids hit Shanika, threw stuff at her and even spit on her. No one would stand next to her, play with her or even touch her, because everybody thought that if you touched Shanika, you would get major cooties. In fact, no one would even talk to her unless it was to insult her. I admit this included me, too. I didn't tease her like the other kids, but I wouldn't stand next to her or touch her.

I felt sorry for Shanika, but I didn't want to completely ostracize myself by being friends with her. Being one of the Jehovah's Witnesses already made me strange enough. One day, Shanika tried to join me at a lunch table, where I was sitting by myself. Even though I had no one else to sit with, I snatched up my tray and moved to another part of the cafeteria. No one was going to accuse me of being friends with Shanika! Looking back, I'm ashamed of the way I treated her. It would be easy now to chalk up my behavior to ignorance and youth, but I was raised better than that, and knew even at that young age that was no way to treat anybody. Shanika acted like she had tough skin, firing back at every insult hurled at her, but I can only imagine what pain we caused her. I think about her today from time to time, wondering how she turned out. I'm sorry she had to go through that trauma.

Not everything was about drama at the Ohrenberger School, however. There were good times as well, like those I spent with my favorite teacher, Mrs. Papahagis. She was truly a darling. She made everything fun, from science to reading and phonics, and she was always kind and helpful. You could tell she truly enjoyed teaching.

I must have really loved Mrs. Papahagis, because I slipped up and called her "Mommy" one day when I was trying to get her attention. The other kids giggled at me. How embarrassing that was! It's funny how you never learn a teacher's first name. I wish I knew it now, so that I could look her up and thank her for her kindness. She was one of the teachers that tried to save me candy and treats from the holiday and birthday parties. I guess she felt sorry for having to exclude me. Even though I longed for the yummy treats and companionship of my peers during the gatherings from which I had to excuse myself, I found a good refuge in the library. When I couldn't participate in the holiday parties, I hung out in there.

It was during the many trips there that I discovered how much I adored books. I had trouble keeping friends, so books became my new friends. In fact, I was one of those kids who got really excited when the Scholastic Books order sheets came around. Even though my mother couldn't afford to order anything for me, I would marvel at the pictures on the book covers. The library gave me the opportunity to read some of those books free of charge.

While there, I became well acquainted with the school librarian, a bubbly, round woman who came into our class once a week to read my favorite childhood series, "Superfudge." "Superfudge" was about a quirky toddler who got himself into weird, often embarrassing, mishaps. The librarian was so animated when she read that each kid clung breathlessly to her every word, only breaking their silence to laugh at one of Fudge's goofy antics. No one dared get up to go to the bathroom, for fear they would miss out on one of his daring escapades.

That was in fourth grade, my last and final year at Ohrenberger. My brother was getting into so much trouble at the Lwellynburg Middle School that my mother had to go there practically every day

Sylvia Coleman

for some sort of parent/teacher conference. She couldn't afford to take off more time from work and she couldn't afford to lose my brother to the streets, so she moved us to the suburbs. We headed to Norwood, Massachusetts.

Chapter 9

Moving to Norwood was a major cultural shock. It was around 1987/1988. At that time, there weren't many black people living there, but with the rapid development of apartment complexes in the area, that started to change. However, before that influx of blacks, we found we were one of the first black families to move into that part of suburbia.

All my life, I had lived mostly around black people, but went to racially diverse schools and congregations, so imagine my surprise upon seeing so many white people in Norwood — and their surprise upon seeing us. I remember one incident when my mother sent me to the local Shaw's grocery store, a white toddler stared me down in the check-out line. The mother quietly took note, beckoning the little girl to stop. But it was too late — the child was clearly captivated by the little brown girl behind her. I innocently thought she was marveling at my eyeglasses, since most kids were intrigued by the large-rimmed bifocals I wore back then.

The mother must have felt embarrassed because she leaned in my direction and said, "I'm sorry she's staring like that. It's just that…she's never seen a black person before." Stunned by her revelation, I tried to manage a smile, but I was speechless. This was perhaps the first time in my life that I became really aware of racial ignorance. I know it sounds strange, but when you grow up in culturally diverse schools and in a culturally diverse congregation, you don't ever take note of these things.

That introduction in the store was mild compared to what was to come later. The town would go to great lengths to remind us of how different we were, but at this point, we were still adjusting to our new surroundings and still making frequent trips to the 'hood to visit our friends. I, for one, really missed my good friend, Melody, and her family.

Since we were on summer break, my mother let me spend the night frequently at Melody's house. She and I were ecstatic! We were like two peas in a pod. Or, maybe I should say three, because we always allowed her little brother, Paul, tag along too. We'd stay out all day playing every game we could think of. It was around this time that I learned how to ride a bike. I was so excited! I even learned some fancy bike stunts. One of my favorite tricks was riding at an angle really low and fast to the edge of the curve. One morning, eager to perform the stunt again, I grabbed a bike and hit the pavement. Paul was out riding too. It seemed like the perfect morning for biking. It was sunny and early, so we could ride freely without too many interruptions from traffic.

But, as the saying goes, it was too good to be true. As I rounded the corner for my finale, I steered the bike too low and skidded onto the road. The bike fell on top of me, crushing my right leg into the gravel on the street. Paul swirled around the corner on his bike, whizzing right past me, giggling. I giggled too. "It's not funny," I exclaimed. However, I was more embarrassed than hurt at the time. As I lay in the street, I saw a car approach. I knew I had to get up and get out of the way fast. I pushed the bike off of me and tried to stand. Pain immediately shot through my right leg as if I were impaled by a sharp object. I looked down and saw a jagged edge of my bone protruding through my skin.

The driver honked his horn. I guess I was moving too slow for him, because he ended up swerving around me. By this time, Paul was coming around the corner again. He was surprised to see me still down on the ground. Fortunately, the neighbor across the street was a nurse and came to my assistance. Melody's Mom, who also was a nurse, came soon afterwards. I had suffered a clean break to my leg and would have to spend the rest of my summer stuck in boring Norwood, where I had no friends.

This was my last visit to the 'hood. A few weeks later, Melody and her family came to visit. I was so excited! We were in my room playing, and her brother, Paul, always the jokester, made a wisecrack about me. I can't remember what he said, but whatever it was, it pissed me off! Before I knew it, I snapped. I picked up my crutch and whacked him in the head so hard that he began bleeding. Everyone looked at me in disbelief. I couldn't believe what I did either! Suffice it to say, that visit was cut short.

Back then, I had a serious attitude. It was hard for people to joke with me because I always took things personally and overreacted. This incident was no different. Even though Paul and I still consider each other family, he has never forgotten that day. He shoots me a dirty glance every time the incident comes up in conversation.

It was also around this time that Melody's Mom, Ernestine, began dating a man named Evan. She worked with him at a local Boston hospital. It seemed like Evan appeared out of nowhere. After a short period of time, he had moved into Ernestine's house. It didn't take a genius to figure out whose bed he was sleeping in, and the situation caused problems between Ernestine and the congregation. Jehovah's Witnesses are not allowed to have sex out of wedlock or date anyone outside of the religion unless that person converts to the faith. Having premarital sex was considered a sin, and Ernestine was warned by the congregation's elders that she could not live that way. But she continued the relationship and soon married Evan. I guess that was the last warning because shortly after, Ernestine was disfellowshipped.

When someone is disfellowshipped from a Jehovah's Witness congregation, that person is cut off from the rest of its members. No one in the congregation is allowed to talk to or associate with that person. If the individual repents, however, he or she can be reinstated to the congregation. For Ernestine to be reinstated, she would have had to divorce her husband, or he would have had to be baptized into the religion. Neither of these things happened, so that visit to our apartment in Norwood was the last time we saw each other as children. My only true friend was now gone, leaving me once again lonely, angry and confused.

Chapter 10

After moving to our new, more expensive apartment in Norwood, my mother had to figure out how to make ends meet, so she worked during the day and went to cosmetology school at night. Living so far away from my father, who still lived in the city, we no longer saw much of him. My brother and I were left to take care of ourselves since our parents were not there. Junior wasn't much of a baby-sitter, so we pretty much went our own separate ways. As I said earlier, my brother was a magnet for trouble, and it didn't take long for trouble to find him this time. He found a new crew in Norwood, and it would lead him to more strife than any of us could imagine.

Meanwhile, I befriended a teenage black girl named Andrea, who lived in our apartment complex. Her family consisted of her Mom, Regina; younger twin sisters, Anya and Tamira; and her mother's live-in boyfriend, Mitch. They became my unofficial "adopted" family. Andrea was about two years my senior, but nevertheless, we soon became best friends. We were the only black girls our age living in the complex and instantly bonded.

I went everywhere with Andrea and her family, and we had lots of fun. Andrea and I did everything together from talking about boys to shopping, gossiping and hanging out. I spent hours in their apartment, from the moment I got home from school until nightfall. To tell you the truth, I don't know how I was able to get any homework done with all the time I spent up there! During the summer, I'd be there from early in the morning until about 8 or 9 p.m. at night. I was over there so much I practically lived there. Andrea's family was originally from Trinidad, but like me, lived in Boston before moving to Norwood. Boston, a culturally diverse city known for its large West Indian population, held an annual Caribbean festival, so every year we would make the trek into the city for the day-long festivities, wearing our best outfits from Marshall's and Tello's.

Andrea was tall for a 14-year-old girl. She was nearly 5 feet 6 inches tall at that time and looked more like a woman than a teen. She was a dark-skin, pretty girl who received a lot of attention from guys and had lots of friends. She was very confident and liked to show it! It was a trait of hers I both admired and envied. In comparison, I was (and still am) 4 feet 11 inches tall. I wore large-rimmed glasses that made my already large eyes look bigger than they were. My lips were entirely too big I felt, and my calves looked like two pin balls.

The more time I spent around Andrea, the more I thought about my appearance. I, too, wanted attention, but felt invisible around her because of her exotic looks. Not that Andrea made me feel bad about my appearance; in fact, she was a great friend and made sure that I went everywhere she and her family went. Yet, somehow in the back of my mind, I thought that if I were prettier I would have more friends, and guys would like me as much as they liked Andrea. Boy, was I ignorant then! Somehow, I always managed to have a falling out with Andrea over stupid things, like her not inviting me somewhere or her hanging out with other friends. But the reality was there were many places I couldn't go with her, because going to those places was against my religion. It's amazing our friendship lasted for as long as it did, considering I always let my jealousy get the best of me.

Andrea also got along extremely well with my mother, which made me even more envious. Frustrated with their tight bond, I found ways to pick a fight with Andrea, so I wouldn't have to see them together. Of course, I wasn't fully aware of my own low self-esteem at the time, but it was causing me and those around me a lot of misery. At that time, no one could have convinced me those silly tantrums were my fault. As far as I was concerned, I was always the victim. When I felt victimized, I retreated and cut off those closest to me. Andrea and other friends put up with that attitude for years, but it was foolish to believe my behavior would go unchecked forever.

Chapter 11

At the same time that I was struggling to maintain my friendship with Andrea, I was having difficulty adjusting to elementary school in Norwood. I had very few friends and was one of only two black kids in the fifth grade.

The next door neighbor, Marissa, also went to my school, but we did not get along. A mean-spirited, freckle-faced bully, Marissa had her mind set on torturing me and always did so when I least expected it. One particular frigid afternoon in January was no exception. I had just gotten off the school bus. Anya and Tamira were walking well ahead of me, and Marissa lingered behind. We exchanged, no doubt, some un-girly words. Caught off guard, she snuck up behind me and shoved me into a towering mound of snow, pinning me down by my neck. I could feel the icy particles seeping into the orifices of my face.

I struggled to get to my feet, but Marissa, who was an overweight girl with broad hands, leaned the entire weight of her body into my back. "Bitch!" she yelled, giving me one last thrust downward. She sprinted off before I could get myself together to chase after her. I felt victimized once again. Something changed in me that day, and I began disliking every white girl I encountered. I began picking fights with anyone who would so much as blink at me the wrong way. I never did get the opportunity to get even with Marissa, so it became easier to take my resentment out on the other white girls around me. It took years for me to abandon that thinking; but at the time, I was blinded by the culmination of old emotional wounds.

Fortunately, things got a little better by the time I got into junior high. I met another black girl named Rochelle Channing, and we became best buddies at school. Having Rochelle as a friend helped a lot — I didn't feel the need to fight as much. I guess like any budding teen, I was trying to find a place where I could fit in with the girls and the boys. I especially wanted to fit in with a boy named John Murphy. He was my first crush. John was in the grade below me and was one of only a handful of black boys at our school. He lived in Windsor Gardens with his Mom and Dad and three other brothers, Manny, Derrick and Jaleel. The Murphy boys were "local celebrities" because their parents had them doing commercials since they were kids. Back then, I was too shy to approach a boy, let alone say "Hi," so I just admired John from a distance.

By the time I mustered enough courage to speak to him, a new girl named Glenda Perez had enrolled in our school and dashed my chances. Glenda was a pretty, tan Latina who had just moved to Norwood with her Mom and brother, Sean. By chance, they just happened to move into the apartment complex where John lived. Soon after Glenda arrived, she and John started dating. Even though John barely knew I was alive, let alone interested in him, I felt hurt and jealous. I talked about how much I liked John to anyone who would listen. I'm sure Rochelle and Andrea grew very tired of my lovesick rantings. But since this was junior high, their relationship was short-lived. I don't know where I got the guts, but I didn't waste any time getting with John. Finally I had a boyfriend I could brag about to Andrea! Somehow that made me feel more worthy of our friendship.

But being a Jehovah's Witness, I wasn't allowed to have a boyfriend, so I had to sneak around to call and see John. I should have known the relationship wouldn't last for long. To my dismay, we only dated for a month or two. Although he never voiced it, I'm pretty sure I was the "rebound chick." Glenda and I were never really friends; we were more like acquaintances. I guess any chance of us being good friends was ruined when I started dating John. Little did we know then, however, that encounter would not be our last connection.

It took me a long time to get over John. He was my first boyfriend, and I was completely infatuated with him. In fact, I vowed to name my firstborn John when I got married. Yeah, I had it really bad for him. Months later, I met a light-skinned Haitian boy named Charles Pierre, who went to an all-boys private school in Westwood, Massachusetts. We met at a dance at his school. Mind you, being a Jehovah's Witness, I was not allowed to go to school dances, but because my mother loved Andrea so much, she trusted me to go out with her. Somehow, I couldn't shake Charles that night. He kept coming back to dance with me, and, before I knew it, we were kissing!

I was too young, foolish and desperate for attention to stop his persistent advances, so I let him feel me up and kiss me right in the open. I gave him my phone number, even though I knew nothing about him. Dumb, huh? Still, he was a boy who was interested in me, and I wanted to have someone to brag about to my friends.

Our relationship was doomed from the very beginning. He lived two towns away, so we only got to see each other once or twice during our seven-month courtship. Realizing it was pointless, I finally convinced Charles it was over. I was so relieved. Even though we were never intimate, Charles was raunchy for a 14-year-old boy. I was too embarrassed to tell him I couldn't even wrap my brain around most of what he asked to do to me.

Chapter 12

During the three years I lived in Norwood, more black people began to move in. I was extremely happy about this change, but unfortunately, not everyone shared my excitement. By the time I made it to eighth grade, trouble was starting to brew between the races.

Fights started to break out more and more between blacks and whites at the high school. Ironically, at the same time, I noticed more and more interracial couples. I don't know if this trend sparked the increase in violence, but there was one incident in particular that left me with no doubt that there was serious racism developing. Someone spray painted: "Niggers fly back to Africa" on the wall outside the school.

It didn't take long for the local media to get wind of the incident, and when the parents of us black students found out, there was utter outrage. Our parents wanted to know who the culprits were and how things had gotten so out of control. To address these demands, the black families agreed to meet. Never in my three years in Norwood had I seen so many black people at one time! Many I hadn't ever seen before.

This was perhaps the only time I saw the black people in Norwood unify. As riled up as the parents were at that meeting, their unification was short-lived. Shortly thereafter, things were back to normal (meaning no more public, blatant expressions of racism), and the black families had resumed daily living.

Personally, I was disgusted by the whole situation. I never truly adapted to my suburban setting and learned to maintain a safe distance from the white kids, talking to them only when necessary.

****

It was right around this time that a kid named Dwight, a fairly new student at the high school, made headlines. His mother, a Boston cop, moved to Norwood to shield him from the increasing violence going on in the city. They moved into one of the older apartment complexes in Norwood, referred to by us black kids as Norwood's "projects" because of its poorly constructed units.

Dwight was well liked at the high school and easily fit in, so you can imagine everyone's distress when they found out he had been shot to death in his own apartment. Apparently, his mother was arguing with her boyfriend, a Boston police detective, when one of them drew a gun. A struggle ensued, and the gun discharged during the brawl. The bullet pierced straight through the wall and struck Dwight in the temple. He died instantly. Ironic, isn't it? Dwight's mother moved him to Norwood to prevent this very thing from happening, only to have him die at her own hand. I never knew what became of his mother or the boyfriend. I can't imagine the amount of guilt she carried after that fateful night.

Chapter 13

While chaos was ensuing across town, we were trying to stop pandemonium from erupting in our own home. Just like the Boston cop who accidentally shot her son, my mother thought moving to Norwood would keep my brother out of danger. How wrong she was! His behavior got significantly worse, especially when he started hanging out with a white kid named Rich Nelson.

Outwardly, Rich seemed like a jovial guy, but he was mischievous. Rich was heavily into drugs, and it didn't take long for Junior to start experimenting with drugs, too. In Boston, black kids stuck to the cheap stuff, like marijuana. In Norwood, it was another story. No drug was off limits. Before long, my brother was hooked, but neither Mom nor I knew it. Ever since Junior and I had stopped sharing a bed, I stayed as far away from him as possible, spending most of my time at Andrea's. And Mom, between working and going to school, wasn't home most of the time.

It seemed as if she could not escape the school's phone calls about her son's unpredictable behavior. Every couple of weeks, Junior was suspended for something different — fighting, back talking or skipping school. Finally, the school had enough and expelled him. He was enrolled in Blue Hill Regional Technical High School a few towns over, but that did not stop him from getting more out of control. Junior missed even more days of school hanging out with Rich. Worse still, items were starting to disappear from our house. When we first noticed our things were missing, we didn't know what was going on. When we finally found out Junior was behind the disappearances, my mother took back his key to the apartment. Still, that didn't stop him. Desperate, he and Rich would climb the balconies leading to our third-floor apartment, pick the lock and make off with our belongings.

The final act of treachery came when he stole our only VCR. My mom used it every day to record her soap operas. Furious, she put him out. I was so thrilled with that decision you would have thought I won the lottery! My mother and I could now live drama-free. However, the peace was short-lived. Junior called and pleaded with Mom to let him come home, and she relented only to kick him out again soon afterwards. This same pattern would continue off and on over the next few months: He'd act up, she'd kick him out, and then she'd inevitably let him come home, not knowing that all the while he was hooked on drugs.

Their constant arguing, fighting and yelling began to take a big toll on me. I remember one evening when I was home alone, Junior staggered in. He stumbled down the hallway, literally falling into the walls. I was so scared I called my mother at work. We later assumed he was buzzing from marijuana, but we didn't know he was high from the potent cocktail of new drugs Rich had introduced him too. When my mother got home that night she tried to beat him, but by this time Junior had grown too tall. She struggled to reach his head to give him a good whack. He was now strong enough to block all of her hits with his forearm. After a few minutes, my mother exhausted all her energy and had to give up.

I often implored Mom to kick him out permanently, but my begging fell on deaf ears. I guess she always thought there was still some hope left for him. Back then, I was constantly accused of being selfish for not wanting to spend time with my brother. But who could blame me? He had molested me, and I did not want to spend a moment more than absolutely necessary with him. But Mom didn't know. I was too ashamed to tell anyone that dirty part of my life. In fact, I had totally suppressed most of my memories from that time when we were younger. To escape our madhouse, I began spending more and more time at Andrea's to the point that even when my mother was home on weekends, I was barely around. All the years my mother worked, studied and chased after my brother had taken an irreparable toll on my relationship with her. We were not close in any sense of the word.

Meanwhile, my brother continued his downward spiral. He was coming in late and running up the phone bill. One time he called a phone sex line and ran the phone bill up close to $1,000! Still, all of these escapades paled to what was yet to come.

****

One evening, while hanging out in the city, Junior was beaten by the Boston police after exiting an MBTA bus. I'm not sure what precipitated this altercation, but I do know he suffered enough blows to the head to land him in the hospital.

Junior was never the same after that. He started hearing voices and said the voices told him to do bad things. My mother believed the head injury and his drug use contributed to his mental demise. Desperate, she sent him to therapy, hoping it would help. He was diagnosed as a paranoid schizophrenic and put on medication that turned him into a walking zombie. I don't think the medicine helped much, because he eventually had to be committed to a psychiatric hospital. The facility was full of more walking zombies. Each patient so heavily drugged all the time that they were barely coherent — including Junior. The patients slept in rooms that had only the basics: a bed, sheets, a lamp and a dresser. Everyone walked around in slippers or lace-free sneakers and pants with no belts. Shoelaces and belts were forbidden for fear the patients would use them to commit suicide.

It was so depressing to see so many unhappy faces. Despite my protest to visiting, Mom made me go with her every weekend to visit Junior. Imagine dragging a 13-year-old to a mental hospital! "What's the point in going?" I asked sarcastically one day. "He's so drugged up he can't even talk to us." Each week I'd leave that place feeling worse than when I came in. I guess Junior felt the same way. He escaped from the mental facility a couple of months later and hitchhiked all the way back to Norwood. I'm not sure if they actually refused to take him back or if my mother just didn't want to send him back, but he never returned to the place.

Chapter 14

Soon after Junior's return, we all took a week-long vacation to Alabama, my mother's home state. I couldn't believe how big my mother's family was! There were three sisters and six brothers.

Including my mother, there were 10 siblings in all. In addition to my aunts and uncles, I met a host of cousins, who ranged in age from toddlers to adults. My mom insisted I had already met many of them during Lisa's funeral, but that was so long ago that I couldn't remember any of their faces. I had tried so hard to forget that time in my life that I subconsciously suppressed a lot of the good memories too, like meeting my mother's siblings.

Everyone in my mother's family had a nickname, including Mom, who was known in those parts as "BeBe" (pronounced "baybay"). The cousins closest to my age were Tony and Donita (Doni), the children of my Aunt Dani (short for Danisha), and Tiffany, the daughter of my Aunt Dee Dee (Deborah). We had a lot of fun meeting all of my mother's people and eating their lip-smacking Southern cooking. Everyone was so excited to see us, especially my grandmother Etta, who I called Granny, my mother's Mom whom they called Maddie. I also enjoyed meeting my great aunts A-Marge (short for Aunt Marge) and A-CeCe (short for Aunt Carolyn).

That week went by too quickly. Soon we were back in Norwood, where Mom now could not stop talking about 'home.' Seeing her family must have really made her miss Alabama because soon thereafter, my mother revealed plans to move there, permanently.

"We're leaving at the end of the school year," she announced.

"Say what?" I retorted.

I liked the South, but I wasn't ready to leave Massachusetts, especially since I was just starting to fit in at Norwood High School. Once again, my petition to stay was dismissed. My mother was resolved to move to Alabama, so by the end of the school year, we packed up all our belongings and drove south. My mother did not have a job or home ready in Alabama, so we stayed with Granny and Grandpa in their trailer. Down south I soon learned, practically everyone either owned or rented a trailer. Since my grandmother had only two extra rooms to spare, I shared a room with my mother. My brother got a room to himself. Not too long after we arrived, my mother obtained a job in a factory about an hour's drive away.

I divided most of my time visiting with my Aunt Lila (Camilla) and hanging out with my cousin, Doni. Lila lived in a trailer across the field from us with her husband, Charlie Joe, and his sons, Putty and Pony, whose real names I never did learn. Lila's house was "comedy central." Everyone over there was wild! Aunt Lila and Charlie Joe were always getting "their drink on." We all thought it was funny, watching them taunt and cuss each other out after some beers.

Looking back now, I can't help but to wonder if they were functional alcoholics.

Perhaps the strangest memory I have of the two of them is their behavior when they returned home late one evening. They shoved each other to get into the trailer, then raced to see who could get to the beer in the refrigerator first! Too young to fully understand the seriousness of their situation, I just laughed at them. Their antics got even crazier when they were inebriated. Uncle Charlie Joe did a comical dance when he got drunk, a weird balancing act that he did on his toes. We nicknamed his crazy dance the Charlie Joe.

Even more amusing than their dancing, was the card games. My relatives would stay up practically all night playing Tonk and Spades. Watching them play cards was better than watching TV. I'd watch them drink all night, slamming their cards down — nearly knocking their empty beer cans off the table. They'd call each other names, cuss each other out and continue their game. Despite their drinking, Aunt Lila and Charlie Joe were actually good people. If anyone ever needed a place to stay, a hot meal or someone to talk to, they were there.

Like I said, if I wasn't at Lila's house, I was hanging with my cousin Doni in the next town over. Doni was what the family called "high yellow" or "red," because her skin color was so light. She was by far the lightest person in our family and very pretty, which, of course, attracted a lot of boys. Virtually every time I spent the night at her house, there was a boy rattling on the door trying to holler at her.

She introduced me to a few of them, but I was too shy to actually go out with any of them. Furthermore, I still wasn't comfortable letting boys get close to me after that long ago encounter with my brother. However, it was nice to get the attention, especially since I was the new girl in town.

By the time I enrolled at the local high school, word had spread that there was a new girl from up north. After a few weeks of school, I was asked out by Darnell, a boy in one of my classes. Darnell was a skinny, light-skinned boy who prided himself on being well-dressed. I'm not sure why I agreed to go out with him, but I did, and our relationship, if you can call it that, lasted only a few weeks. Living the next town over, I barely got a chance to see him. Besides, I think he was more interested in being the first to date the new girl in school than anything else.

Meanwhile, I developed friendships with several of my classmates, including Ronetta and Bonetta Logan, my twin neighbors down the street. Although I hung around both, and both were equally entertaining, Ronetta and I became especially close. Somehow, the conversations with Ronetta and Bonetta always centered on the latest gossip and boys. They boasted like guys about their own sexual escapades. Some folks may have been put off by this talk, but I always thought they both were really cool! I mean, as young as they were, they knew the in's and out's of dating and weren't afraid to be blunt about what they knew. Especially Ronetta. Social by nature, she could command an audience of listeners effortlessly. Somehow, she always seemed older than what she really was.

If I wasn't with the Logans or my family, I was attending the Kingdom Hall. When we lived in Norwood, I went by myself. My mother always arranged to have someone pick me up for Sunday service and the weekly Bible study. But when we moved to Alabama, a local neighbor, whose son went to my high school, began picking me up. Everything was cool in the beginning, but as time passed, it became more and more challenging for me to be devoted to the religion. There was so much peer pressure around me, even more so than when I had lived up North in Massachusetts.

As time went on, I met several teens from my school in the congregation, and I learned that all of them led double lives. I would see them exit the Kingdom Hall and start cussing as soon as they got outside. The guys there talked just as crudely about girls as the boys in school. Even my close friend, Janet, who I also met through the congregation, was leading a double life. Janet lived in Greenville, a nearby town. She had slanted eyes and was even lighter than my cousin Doni. In fact, as her mother tells it, the Asian doctor that delivered Janet was convinced her mom had given birth to a Chinese baby! With such exceptional looks, Janet was heavily pursued by boys, and her mother knew it. Her mom would warn her, "Don't come home with any babies!" That summer, Janet went to visit her father in California and came back pregnant.

With all this hypocrisy going on around me, it's amazing I too didn't jump on the romance bandwagon right away. For a while, however, I kind of lived in the shadows of my friends, watching them go out and date and vicariously living through their wacky exploits. However, it didn't take long for me to build a social life that rivaled theirs. More boys started to approach me, and I began getting more attention than I had ever received before. My biggest suitors were Rick, a quiet, church-going type; Mason, a chubby, comical sweetheart; and Mitchell, a light-skinned lady's man who had dated Doni. Against all common sense, I passed on the "good guys" for Mitchell — but not before I got the okay from Doni. Mitchell was funny, charming and a great kisser! Everything seemed to be cool with us, so I just rolled with the relationship.

Meanwhile, my mother's car conked out, so she couldn't continue her job in the factory. Things were starting to get really rough for us. At the same time, my mischievous brother was acting up again. Unable to control his erratic behavior and adapt to our new environment, he went back to Massachusetts. My mother soon followed to help him.

As for me, I was spending more and more time at Lila's house, mainly to use her phone. We didn't have a phone in my grandmother's trailer, so I had to take all of my calls over there. Most of those calls came from Mitchell. Around this time, my cousin Pony started to take an interest in me. At first it seemed innocent — he would compliment my outfit or say my hair looked nice. But then he would try to corner me in bedrooms or in the bathroom, whispering vulgar things to me about what he wanted to do to me sexually. In the beginning, I managed to stave off his advances, but he persisted. He finally ambushed me in a corner of my Aunt Lila's bedroom and tried to feel me up. I managed to break free, but was too ashamed to tell anyone, especially after hearing rumors about what he had done to a girl in the next town over. That girl, barely a teen, claimed he had raped her, but it was her word against his, and Pony denied any wrongdoing. The general consensus in the family favored Pony's version of events. Knowing this, I thought it best to keep quiet about my encounter.

After that incident in the bedroom, I dramatically cut back my visits to Lila's house. Every now and then, they questioned why I hadn't been over as much. I went about my business, thinking I had gotten rid of Pony for good. One night I was jolted from sleep by pounding on my bedroom window. Pony knew my mother was still away in Boston, so he had taken advantage of this time to continue harassing me. He stood outside banging on the window for what seemed like a half hour, harassing me to let him in. Unbelievable, I thought to myself! I lay as still as I could. I didn't want to risk him hearing me. If I hadn't known before how imperative it was to keep my distance from him, I knew so now. This fool was crazy!

I never knew when he was going to pop up. Sometimes he would make ridiculous excuses to come to my grandmother's house where I lived. Although they were brief visits, I made sure to exit the room or ignore him altogether. Little did I know how sneaky Pony could get. One day, one of my little cousins ran to Granny's house to tell me I had a phone call from Mitchell. I quickly dashed across the field to my Aunt Lila's house. When I got there, no one was on the line. I phoned Mitchell and asked him if he had called, and he told me he hadn't. That was strange, I thought, but we chatted for a couple of minutes and got off the phone.

Just as I was about to exit Lila's room, Pony stepped into the doorway, admitting it was he who had lured me over there with the fake message. Bewildered, all I could think about was how to get out of there. It was too late. Pony closed the door and pinned me to the bed, tightening his grip. He jammed his tongue into my mouth.

"You want this. Admit it!" he demanded, as I tried to dodge his lips.

I begged him to let me go. There was no one there. No one could hear me. Finally, he ceased trying to kiss me and released one of his hands. Whew! I assumed he was letting me go. Hardly, Pony worked his way down to my chest and in between my thighs, ramming his fingers into me. I squirmed in his tight grip trying to wiggle my hands free, but the more I fought, the more forceful he became, bearing down with his weight and wrenching his fingers deeper inside me. My pelvis began to ache. Impulsively, he moved his head down to my waist. I began to panic. My legs were now trembling uncontrollably. What was he doing? Within seconds, I found out; but it was hard for him to keep holding my arms down and maintain his head below my waist, so I took this opportunity to break free.

I know I must have looked a mess bolting from that trailer with my clothes all disheveled, but I didn't care. I sprinted like someone was chasing me with a gun. In fact, I didn't stop running until I reached the bathroom door inside our trailer. Immediately, I hurried into the shower, but all the scrubbing and soap could not erase the stench of Pony from my mind. I was so sore from that encounter that I was barely able to wipe myself with tissue in the bathroom.

Around this time, I went into a self-imposed exile. I never went over to Lila's house for anything. So, of course, my boyfriend Mitchell started to wonder what was going on when he couldn't reach me on Lila's phone. He managed to hitch a ride into town to see me one evening, and I described the dreadful encounter I had had with Pony. Mitchell was so furious, he wanted to go over there and pummel him. It took a while for me to get him to calm down, but we didn't have much of an evening after that. Talking about Pony had really gotten to me, and I didn't feel too good about myself anymore.

Somehow I felt I was to blame for the incident, and I began feeling more and more ashamed of my body — so much so that I had a hard time being intimate with Mitchell over the next several weeks. He was the first guy I had actually given myself permission to be with in that way, but after what happened at Aunt Lila's, I could not stomach being touched. It wasn't Mitchell's fault that I felt so dirty, but still the feelings persisted. I guess our break-up was inevitable.

Chapter 15

It seemed as if everyone in my family had undergone some type of drama. One day, while watching TV with my grandparents, we were startled by a loud rattling vibration outside our trailer. We dashed outside, astounded by what we saw.

Choppers were circling the field adjacent to the trailer. Hummers were approaching the house at breakneck speed, kicking up dirt and rocks in their path. They were still some distance away, but it was clear the men in these vehicles were armed. In fact, it looked as if they were ready for an all out attack! Almost like something out of a movie, only the movie was taking place right in front of our house.

Bewildered by what was going on, I stood dazed. Before I could ask Granny what was happening, she had disappeared across the street to my Uncle Beany's house. Everyone was moving fast, scurrying around like hunted prey. Granny then jetted over to Aunt Dee Dee's house, which I thought was odd, because we all knew Dee Dee was at work. Granny and my uncle were shuffling around at Dee Dee's for a good few minutes before the brigade of armed men closed in. In retrospect, I think these men were from the U.S. Bureau of Alcohol, Tobacco and Firearms (ATF), but at that age I didn't know who they were or what was going on.

They entered my uncle's house and exited soon after, roaming his backyard for a long time. Eventually they emerged with bags of something. I wanted to run over and get a closer look, but Granny demanded I stay put. She tried to play it cool, but I could see the anxiety building on her face. The remaining men emerged with my Uncle Beany in handcuffs. Granny hobbled down the steps toward them. It was clear they were shouting, but I couldn't make out what they were saying because of the loud engines and helicopters still circling overhead. Defenseless, my grandmother retreated to the house, and the men exited.

Uncle Beany did not come home for a while. I later learned he was arrested for growing marijuana in his yard, and when the armed brigade busted him, he and Granny had raced to Aunt Dee Dee's to flush some of it down her toilet. I don't know whose drugs they were, but it was a well-known fact that my aunt was having an affair with the county's biggest drug dealer, Mickey D. Uncle Beany ended up doing time in jail. Of course, my family tried to conceal all of it from us kids, but it was hard to keep a secret like that under wraps. The idyllic impressions I had of my mother's family were suddenly beginning to fade.

As time went on, I realized my family was marred by many salacious secrets. My uncle James was cheating on his sweet wife, Farrah. My cousin Putty was sleeping with his uncle's sister-in-law, and my five-year-old cousin, Brickey, was addicted to chewing tobacco.

****

My mother eventually came back from Boston alone. Thinking things would get better without my brother around to upset the family, we tried to resume a "normal" life. However, relationships begin to slowly deteriorate within my mother's family. There was a lot of jealousy and resentment brewing between the siblings, but I could not figure out why.

Around this time, my mother began to complain more and more of having headaches. We thought they were just migraines, so she'd pop an aspirin and lie down. One night while experiencing a migraine, she did just that, and we went to bed. Within minutes of turning off the light, I heard a loud shriek. I leapt to my feet and flung on the light, alarmed by what I saw. My mother was shaking violently and her jaw was clinched shut.

"Ma! Ma!" I yelled, but she did not respond. Her eyes had rolled back into her head. Fortunately I recalled having heard about something called a seizure a couple of years earlier when a female rapper named MC Trouble had died from one. They described her as having the same symptoms Mom was having. It was said they tried to use a spoon to pry the rapper's mouth open, so I grabbed a spoon from the kitchen and attempted to do the same. When this didn't work, I ran to get Granny from her bedroom. She sent me to get Aunt Lila, who worked in a nursing home. I was terrified. All I could think was, God, don't let anything happen to my mom. Normally I wouldn't cross the field to Lila's house at night due to the snakes in those deep country woods, but on this occasion I was in such a state of panic that I bolted through the field as fast as I could!

I rattled on Aunt Lila's door for several minutes before she finally emerged. By this time, Granny had gotten Aunt Dee Dee too, and we all piled into the car and took Mom to the hospital in the next town over. This particular hospital was more like a clinic, to be honest. They were able to stabilize my mother, but then had to fly her in an emergency helicopter to a bigger hospital in Montgomery, Alabama so she could get proper treatment. My mother was hospitalized for the next couple of days. As it turned out, she had had a grand mal seizure. The doctor could not pinpoint the cause, but prescribed Dilantin® and said she would have to take it the rest of her life. My mother did not like hearing that news at all.

After her near-death experience, the family seemed to pull a little closer together to take care of her. Things got back on track. Truth be told, I loved my extended family and wanted to see them be on better terms. Unfortunately, whatever peace we could find was short lived. Slowly, dissension began to divide the family again. No one in the family spoke to each other, and you could feel the tension when you walked into the room, so much so that my mother moved us into Aunt Lila's house. Great, I thought, just where I needed to be.

We only stayed there for a short time before my mother decided it was time to move back to Boston. While we were there I never stayed in the house alone with Pony. I was both relieved and nervous about moving back to Boston. My mother didn't have a job or any money, but she was determined to get as far away from her family as possible. When we got back to Boston, we ended up at my friend Andrea's house in Norwood. Her mother was kind enough to put us up for a couple of days. From there, we went to Mattapan, where Frederick, my cousin Tiffany's father, lived. We stayed with him for a few days. Then my grandmother called asking us to return to Alabama.

****

We returned on a train and moved back into Granny's. I re-enrolled in school. Things seemed to get a little better, but there was still tension between Mom and her siblings. According to her, some of her siblings resented the fact that she was allowed to live in that trailer rent-free. The only person my mother truly stayed cool with was her sister, Lila. It didn't take long for things to fall apart once again. After a few weeks, no one was on speaking terms in that trailer. My grandparents moved back into their old house across the street, and shut off the electricity in the trailer. We had to live by candlelight.

Not too long afterwards, my grandmother sent over a handwritten note demanding we leave her property at the end of the school year. To say my mother was livid is an understatement, but she was powerless. It was Granny's property, and we had no choice but to leave. All this strife among the adults in Mom's family put a strain on my relationship with my cousins. Sadly, we didn't talk much. I was really hurt by that situation because I wanted to have a bond with my mother's family.

As the school year wound down, I began saying good-bye to my new friends. No one could believe I was leaving, especially my sweet friend, Mason, who had had a crush on me since the beginning of the year. When school ended in May, Mom put our biggest stuff in storage, and we left. We only had enough money to take the train to Birmingham. There we checked into a Salvation Army shelter downtown.

Chapter 16

I wasn't too keen about living in a shelter, especially sharing a space with other people I did not know. Since this was a family shelter, each room housed two families. My mother and I kept to ourselves as much as possible, but I befriended one of the staff volunteers, a teenager about my age. My mother became friends with a woman down the hall who had two children, a preteen girl and a teenage boy. My mother liked the fact that the woman's children were well behaved. We got along great with them but couldn't help notice something strange about the mother and son. Our suspicions were confirmed weeks later when someone caught the mother showering with her son. She shrugged the incident off as "normal" and chastised anybody who thought otherwise. After that incident, we spent less time with them.

A few weeks later, the shelter moved us into a unit adjacent to the shelter, which was essentially a mini-apartment with two bedrooms. Meanwhile, we tried to spend as much time as possible outside of the shelter. Birmingham was a beautiful city, but not really exciting. We would ride the trolley or stroll in the park to pass time. One day, we were walking in a local park near the shelter and ran into some unwelcomed "excitement." Marching toward us with bullhorns and racist signs was a large group of skinheads and Klu Klux Klan members. Never had I expected to see such a sight in my lifetime. At that time it was 1992! I thought those groups no longer existed. No doubt my mother had flashbacks of the 1960s, because she began walking so fast in the opposite direction that I could barely keep up. After that encounter, we called it a day and headed back to the shelter, where she was convinced now more than ever that it was time to get the hell out of the shelter in Alabama.

It was around this time that one of the counselors suggested we seek help from the local Kingdom Hall down the street. Mom was initially reluctant since she had felt betrayed by the congregation near her hometown when she'd asked for help a few weeks earlier. But we were in no position to refuse assistance, so we visited the congregation. After a long discussion with the congregation elders, they agreed to lend her some money. It wasn't much but, along with more funds from the United Way, their money enabled us to take an Amtrak train to Boston. Mom reasoned that if we were going to be homeless, we might as well be homeless in a place we knew. She figured it would be easier to secure a job in Boston since the economy was better in the North.

****

The first shelter we stayed at in Boston was Pine Hall, a true hellhole! All the homeless slept in a large, gymnasium-size room on single cots. You definitely had to watch your possessions in that shelter. Most people slept with their belongings tucked under them. In the morning, everyone had to leave because the shelter had a rule that no one could lounge or loiter around the place during the day. This ordinance, I reasoned, explained the large number of homeless people I'd see roaming the Boston streets in the daytime.

My mother knew this shelter was no place to raise a child, so she began seeking better accommodations. She found a three-story house that had been converted into a family shelter. Each bedroom held its own family. Thank God there were just the two of us — some families had to sleep four or five to a bedroom! This place was much nicer than Pine Hall, but I still longed for my own bedroom and a place we could call home. We had moved so much in the last year that I was physically and emotionally exhausted. By this time, school was about to start. I was going into the 11th grade, so my mother enrolled me into Brighton High. I had to take several forms of transportation to get there.

Things were okay in the beginning at the shelter, but chaos soon unfurled. My mother had verbal confrontation after confrontation with other residents and the staff. I tried to get her to tone it down. "I know some of the things they do around here isn't right, but I don't want to move again," I begged her, but once again, my input was disregarded. Mom was not good at holding her tongue. She scoffed at the repeated written warnings, as if daring the shelter to kick us out.

Looking back, I think she was just as frustrated and depressed about our living situation as I was and instead took out her frustration on the people in the shelter.

Finally they had enough of my mom's unpredictable behavior. One day, I came back to the shelter from school to find our belongings out on the porch. We were officially terminated. I stood there, sobbing in the barrage of rain that was now saturating my clothes. Where would we go? What would we do? How would I get to school? Would we have to sleep outside in the cold rain? I was scared. My mind was filled with the worst scenarios possible.

I don't know how or who called who, but the next thing I knew, we were heading to Ernestine's house in the projects. I was both delighted and nervous about this move. We hadn't seen them in years. When we arrived, however, my fears dissipated. Everyone was excited to see us. It was as if our friendship had never ended. However, their family had grown considerably. They now had three more siblings, Little Evan and Little Ernestine. These were children Ernestine had had with Evan after they married. A third sibling was Evan's daughter Michelle from his previous marriage. With all these people living in the house, it's amazing they even had any room for us. We stayed for a few weeks. Even though it was crowded, I felt at home. I was elated to have hot cooked meals and a familiar roof over my head. But as the saying goes, all good things must come to an end. Ernestine was doing us a favor, and we knew we couldn't take advantage forever. If the Boston Housing Authority had found out there were two families living there, we could have all been tossed out! Still, I relished every minute I had with them.

When we left, we moved to the YMCA on Huntingdon Avenue, adjacent to Northeastern University. This main branch of the YMCA provides shelter for homeless adults and families. It was a very clean shelter, but once again, the living quarters were cramped. My mother and I shared a bunk bed — she was on the bottom, me on top. Fortunately, the food was pretty good, and we received a lot of really nice donations, so we didn't have to worry about basic necessities.

I met another girl named Faye Marie there, who also went to Brighton High. She was in a grade below me, but was instrumental in helping me adjust. Plus, it felt good knowing I wasn't the only homeless kid going there. Although I got to know a few people at school, I kept to myself mostly because I didn't want people to know I lived in a shelter. I really didn't fit in either. All my clothes were from Goodwill, and my hair was definitely not hooked up like that of the other girls. Tired of looking so poor, I decided to look for work. I landed my first job at Taco Bell across the street from the shelter.

I worked for a loud and boisterous, young Jamaican woman. I was so happy to be employed that I didn't pay her too much attention at first. I was also digging the fact that I got to eat lunch there for free! Slowly, however, my manager started to show her true colors, coming undone whenever we had a mob of customers. When she panicked, she became very condescending toward us employees. I tried my best to stay out of her way, but being the youngest and the only other female, I became an easy target. As if her lengthy rantings were not enough, she began having me run her personal errands. On more than one occasion, I had to deliver food to men in the area that she liked. Nevertheless, I continued to work there. Sadly, I had gotten used to being the victim.

Meanwhile, Mom began having problems at this shelter, too. It seemed like every time I turned around she was confronting somebody or filing complaints against someone. She and I constantly argued over this issue. Of course, she was always right and I was wrong. This tension began to slowly erode our relationship. I don't recall if we were kicked out or just asked to leave, but I do know we had to make an unexpected exit. It wasn't a surprise, considering my mother's previous history with shelters.

We ended up in a shelter out in Lynn, Massachusetts, a town on the outskirts of Boston. Our new abode was a motel that had been converted into a shelter for families. Perhaps the only good thing about this place was that Mom and I each got our own full-size bed and dresser. We had a nice big color TV too and didn't have to share our bathroom with other residents. The only downside was the public transportation. It ran slowly in Lynn, which meant a longer commute to school for me.

Although our accommodations were better, it did little to improve our relationship. One evening all hell broke loose. I can't tell you what we argued about, but I think we both snapped, because my mother and I were tumbling around the room in an all-out brawl — smacking, hitting and pushing each other. I couldn't believe it! It was as if I were watching someone else fight with their parent. Up until then, I had always been too afraid of Mom to attempt any retaliation. I guess there was still some fear in me though because as soon as I broke free from her grip, I scampered into the bathroom and locked the door behind me.

"Get out of that bathroom!" her voice bellowed on the other side of the door. "I want you outta here!" Suddenly I realized my mother was not just trying to get me out of the bathroom, but out of the shelter and away from her. Too frightened to come out, I stayed holed up in the bathroom until I heard her leave the following morning. I didn't waste any time packing my stuff. I didn't know where I was going, but I knew I was getting the hell out of there and not coming back. I ended up at my Aunt Mae's apartment. Mae, who was actually my uncle's long-time girlfriend, lived in the South End section of Boston. She was kind enough to let me stay, but she did tell my mother and my father, who I hadn't seen in years, that I was staying with her.

Chapter 17

Believe it or not, in the midst of this calamity there was a glimpse of hope. My attitude and living situation dramatically improved at Mae's house. It felt great being away from all the drama, plus, my high school guidance counselor informed me that I had been accepted into the MassPep Summer Engineering Program at Wellesley College in Wellesley, Massachusetts.

I wasn't interested in engineering, but I was still excited because I would have something to do with my summer and receive a stipend for attending. I was even more excited to learn that several people I knew from school would be going too. There was Ethel; my friend Riana; and Barry, a dark-skinned track runner from my homeroom. In addition to us Brighton High kids, there were students from schools all over Boston, including the prestigious Cambridge Ridge and Latin High School. There was even a girl named Tina from Texas.

The program lasted for about six weeks. We lived on campus Monday thru Friday and came home on weekends. On our first day, we met our three counselors — Temple, Khalid and Ray. They gave us our class schedules and went over the program rules. By that evening, we were off on our own. Of course everyone was trying to feel each other out, so we decided to play "Truth or Dare." Sometime during the school year, I had developed a little crush on Barry back in homeroom at Brighton High, but he was dating a very overbearing chick named Sherry, so I hid my feelings. Still, we remained cordial, and Barry was always polite to me.

My feelings for Barry seemed to heighten when we got to MassPep, but I was still too shy to speak up. I laid low, deciding to take the subtle route and I waited to see if he felt the same way about me. I guess I was a little too subtle, because Tina made it quite clear that she was interested in Barry too. Apparently, a few people had developed crushes, because everyone became eager to play "Truth or Dare" and let those attractions be known. Someone did ask if I liked Barry during that game, but somehow I managed to worm my way out of responding. I didn't want to play myself in front of everybody, especially Barry. After the game was over, I couldn't help but think all hope was loss to make my feelings known to him. Soon after that game, Barry and Tina started dating.

Although the two of them were together, there was a connection between Barry and me that neither of us could shake. Yes, he was with another girl, but it was quite obvious when we were in each other's presence that there was a mutual attraction. Because there was little I could do about my feelings, I tried to redirect my focus to other parts of the program. Overall, our classes were great. Although I struggled through math, the combined workload from all the classes wasn't that bad. I really excelled in the writing class. In fact, I won a place in a national poetry contest the teacher entered for us. My winning poem, "Dear Mommy," was about an unborn child pleading for his life while his teenage mom was waiting in a clinic to have her abortion. I'm not sure how I came up with that one! I always was a deep thinker and had what my family called "an old soul." That poem was probably the true beginning of my interest in writing.

As much as I enjoyed the classes, I also craved the downtime. I didn't have cable at my aunt's house, so I would squeeze every free moment I had in the student lounge, watching videos on BET. Back then, SWV, Onyx and Jodeci were in heavy rotation. When I wasn't watching videos, I was busy hanging with my girl Riana. Riana, who is half Honduran and half West Indian, was what the guys considered a hot chick. At just 15, she was turning the heads of both boys and men, and she knew it. She definitely used her overdeveloped physique to her advantage. Combined with her intellectual prowess and super-cool demeanor, Riana was liked by everyone.

She was also very comical and sharp-witted. If you tried to bust on her, she had a response before you could finish your sentence. She and I spent hours gossiping, laughing and talking about the guys. Although I didn't have much to report on that front, I did give great advice, and so became a confidant to many (and still am today). However, I wore her ear off talking about Barry, wondering what he was doing and if he was thinking about me. In case you haven't figured it out, I had "it" really bad for the guy.

When I wasn't discussing my problems with Riana, I was shooting the breeze with my program counselor, Khalid. He and I became pretty tight, rapping about everything. Khalid was five years older than me, but we communicated as if we had known each other for years. He gave me great advice on everything from selecting a college to choosing a man. Some started to speculate that we were more than friends, but for the most part, we just ignored the rumors and continued to hang out. On some subconscious level, I think there was a bit of an attraction between Khalid and me. One evening, while we were taking a stroll, we ended up in a secluded part of the campus and came very close to kissing. I guess Khalid must have come to his senses, because he stopped about a half-inch from my lips. "Nah, I can't do this. It's not right."

As much as we were both "feeling each other" in that moment, I had to admit he was right. He and I could have gotten into trouble. Besides, I was still underage, so we decided it was best not to start something we couldn't finish. On the one hand, it was great that I had finally taken an interest in somebody other than Barry, who was still with Tina. I knew though there was no future for me and Khalid. Besides my being underage, Khalid went to school in Florida and would be going back at the end of the summer. We decided to keep what almost happened to ourselves and never took another late night stroll.

Almost everyone on the campus was hooking up. That is, everyone but me. Through it all, I guess I never stopped liking Barry. Toward the end of the program, he and I finally admitted how much we liked each other. Ironically, his relationship was falling apart with Tina. He said she had become too bossy. Barry and I continued our relationship after MassPep. Fortunately, we lived within walking distance of each other in Boston. Barry and I were never physically intimate, but we did enjoy long walks around the city, arm in arm. To tell you the truth, our relationship was too short lived to be intimate. Besides, I don't think I was ready for that step. I still had a hard time being close to guys after what my brother and cousin had put me through. Though I know he wanted to take our relationship to the next level, Barry remained a perfect gentleman the whole time we were together.

A couple of nights I came home a little late, not much, but just enough to cause Mae to worry. She began to get paranoid, saying Barry was causing me to act out. I apologized, trying to explain what a great guy Barry was, but she was not trying to hear it.

"Are you having sex with this guy?" she blurted out.

This woman must be crazy, I thought. Realizing we were never going to see eye to eye on Barry, I stopped arguing with her. She was so desperate to end my relationship with Barry that she called my father over to talk to me about it. He gave me a short lecture about dating and obeying my aunt. But, all the while, I kept thinking, who is he to tell me what to do after all of these years of being M.I.A.? Still, I remained respectful until he left. That was the last time I saw him. From that day forward, things were strained between Mae and me. We barely spoke but it was a hell of a lot better than arguing. I figured I could live that way to keep the peace between us. Just when I thought Mae was done harassing me about Barry, she dropped a major bombshell one evening.

"I heard that boy is a drug dealer around here."

"What!" I could hardly believe what was coming out her mouth!

"Who told you that lie?"

"The neighbors down the street told me all about him."

"Well, they told you wrong," I said, defending him. "Anyone who really knows Barry knows that's not even in his character. He's too obsessed with running track to be selling some drugs. Plus his mother don't play that."

Still convinced the wild story was true, Mae repeated the tale to my mother. I hadn't seen much of Mom since coming to live with Mae. There was still a lot of bad blood between us. She was actively dating a Latino man she had met in the shelter out in Lynn. It was her first relationship since leaving my father years ago. After a few months in the shelter, they got an apartment together in a Dorchester housing project. I didn't realize Mae had told my mother, so imagine my astoundment when I came home one day and she was there. At first, I didn't know she was there. I walked in, and Mae began interrogating me with a lot of weird questions about Barry. Suddenly, my mother jumped out from Mae's bedroom, shouting at me.

"You're coming to live with me, and I am not going to let you out of my sight! And, you're going to stop seeing that boy. In fact, you're going to come straight home from school, do your homework and that's it!"

I was angry, stunned and heartbroken all at the same time. I can't recall whose car we piled my stuff in to go to her place. I think it was Ernestine's. I do remember it was raining heavy. My mother lectured me all the way to her apartment. I kept trying to explain that Mae was wrong about Barry but she was not trying to hear it. By the time we arrived at her place, I had made up my mind. I could not live with her. My relationship with Barry was not going to suffer over some preposterous lie. When the car stopped, I jumped out, grabbed as much of my stuff as I could carry, and darted as fast as I could away from the car.

"Come back here!" my mother bellowed in my direction.

I could not believe what I was doing. Before the fight we had had in the hotel, I had never disobeyed my mother — I was always too scared to. I had no clue where I was going. I just wanted to get as far away from her as possible. Thank God, I had the presence of mind to call my good friend Rolanda and her family. I explained what had happened, and they told me to come straight over. Rolanda was originally from North Carolina and had just graduated from Brighton

High. She was one of the few people I became really close to at the school, and her family and I got along great. Her mother was a beautiful, tall caramel woman who looked like a supermodel. However, she had advanced-stage diabetes and was always in and out of the hospital. Rolanda and her mother's roommate took turns taking care of her.

Her mother had an extremely pleasant disposition. In many ways, she thought of me as her own daughter and wouldn't hear of me living on the streets. At first I thought she was just letting me stay for a few nights, but after about a week or so, she insisted I move in permanently. I reluctantly declined. Perhaps I had too much pride. My decision really troubled her, but she understood how much I wanted a place of my own.

Rolanda's Mom was a former social worker and insisted on helping me find a suitable living environment. She suggested Bridge Over Troubled Waters. Even though she was feeble and plagued with pain from her illness, she insisted on taking me there personally. I will never forget that day. We took public transportation, and although Bridge was just a few short blocks from the subway, the walk was extremely difficult for her. She was feeling particularly sick that day and could barely walk. The diabetes had clearly ravaged her body and her vision, because she could not see very far in front of us. "You don't have to go on," I told her, but she insisted completing the final leg of the journey. She wanted to get me there safely. She clung to my arm, as we walked arm in arm to Bridge. Every few steps we had to stop so she could catch her breath, sit and rest. When we arrived, I met with Bridge counselors. They agreed to give me emergency shelter at a place called Trinity, which was actually a rectory attached to a church that had been converted to a homeless shelter/group home for teens. The next day, I moved in.

Chapter 18

Trinity was one of the first teen group homes in the United States. It was a narrow edifice with four floors. The first level housed a restaurant-style kitchen and an adjoining living room; the second floor was the boys' dormitory; floor three was the staff office and TV room; and level four was the girls' living quarters.

There were strict rules at Trinity. Curfew was 10 p.m. Everyone was assigned a different daily chore, as well as a cooking day when you had to make dinner for the 15-20 residents in the group home. You also had an assigned day to go grocery shopping with the staff to prepare for your meal. Everyone was given three weekly counselors: One for family therapy, another for in-house counseling and the third for personal counseling at Bridge headquarters downtown. In addition to meeting with these three counselors, there was a mandatory Tuesday night group meeting. Those with addictions also had to attend a 12-step group. Residents were required to work, maintain a budget and pay a weekly $50 rent. And, last but not least, residents were not allowed to date each other.

I could live with the chores and dinner responsibilities, but I wasn't too keen on the counselor thing. I couldn't understand why we had so many counselors, nor did I understand why I needed a family therapist since I did not have any intentions to reconcile with my mother. Besides, all of the counselors at Trinity were white, and I was convinced they would not understand my experience. What's more, I couldn't foresee telling my personal business to someone I didn't know. I still held a lot of resentment toward white people from my days in Norwood. As far as I was concerned, these white people at Bridge were no different. I told all of this to a white counselor named Ryan, and he looked astonished and turned beet red. All he could think to say was that I had to learn to trust the counselors and that the first three months would be the toughest trying to adjust to my new environment.

"We'll see," I said, rolling my eyes at him. I was determined to keep them at arm's length. My two counselors at the downtown headquarters were Kate, a white woman who was my family counselor; Willard, a blind black man who was my personal counselor; and Tammy, a short, curly-haired woman who worked as my in-house counselor. From the moment I met these counselors, I resolved not to like or trust any of them, especially Tammy because of her brazen personality. I decided to keep to myself, but the staff seemed determined to break the stubborn demeanor I expressed around them.

While I didn't care much for the counselors, I did get along great with my roommates: Theresa, a Puerto Rican girl who bared a striking resemblance to the Mexican singer Selena; Tracy, a short West Indian girl; and Ellen, a heavyset white girl. I'll never forget the first day I met them and the "surprise" they had for me.

"Are you going to tell her?" Theresa said to Ellen.

"Tell her what?" Ellen replied.

"You know ——."

"Honest to, God, Theresa! I was going to get around to it!" Ellen shot back at her.

"Well, either you tell her or I will. I mean, she should know since she's now your roommate," she argued back.

"Tell me what?" I interjected.

"I'm gay," Ellen blurted out.

"Oh," I replied, "Is that it? I already knew that!"

"Do you have a problem with it?" asked Ellen.

"No," I said. "We're cool just as long as we respect each other's privacy. I mean, I don't think you would try to do anything to me. Plus, who's to say I'm your type?"

I guess my feelings about Ellen being gay broke the ice because they all cracked up laughing. For the most part, I got along great with the residents. In fact, one of my closest friends in the shelter was a gay Jamaican brother by the name of Walt. Walt was a trip. He was smart and comical, but like the rest of us Bridge residents, he had issues too. He was dating a man who was studying to be a Catholic priest.

Sylvia Coleman

****

By this time, my senior year had started, and I had just landed a job at Au Bon Pain, a local French cafe. I went to school, worked, paid rent, did chores and maintained my curfew. Still, I remained resistant to therapy, especially with Kate and Tammy. And even though I did not have an addiction, they told me I had to choose a 12-step program. Come again? I couldn't worm my way out of it so I started going to Overeaters Anonymous with Ellen, just to get them off of my back. I never did understand what the heck was going on in those meetings, but I went anyway. Some residents had to attend two to three of these 12-step meetings a week. How they fit those meetings in with the busy tasks the group home had us doing, I don't know. My schedule was hard enough for me to handle. In fact, it was so jam packed that I hardly had time to see Barry.

Even though I dreaded going to work, my co-workers made it fun, especially Steve. He went to Madison Park High School in Roxbury, Massachusetts. Steve was always doing or saying something silly to make me laugh. He was also a big flirt and joked around about wanting to take me out. At least I thought he was joking, since he knew I had a boyfriend. In fact, they both lived in the same housing complex, so they were well acquainted. I talked about Barry all the time while I was at work, which seemed to annoy Steve. After a couple of months, I learned to ignore his flirting. Honestly, I never took him seriously because he made advances so frequently that it just became a normal part of shift banter. Plus, it had taken Barry and me a long time to get together, so Steve should have known I wasn't about to break up any time soon. I guess I underestimated Steve, because he did not give up without a fight.

One evening we went about our normal routine to close the store. Steve usually carried all the heavy stuff down to the basement, and I managed restocking upstairs. One night he called me down to the basement, saying he needed help with something. I hated going down those stairs because they were narrow steel steps, so I gave him a lot of lip about making me do extra work.

"What do you want Steve?" I bellowed from the top of the stairs. "I'm ready to go home."

I looked around and did not see him. Just as I turned to head back upstairs, Steve grabbed me by the waist, spun me around and pressed his lips against mine. I seized the railing to back away, but he pulled me in closer. I was stunned yet, surprised that Steve was such a good kisser! Finally, I broke free from his grip, sprinted upstairs, grabbed my stuff and hurried out the door. All I could think about was Barry. What would he say? What would he think? What did this mean for us? As nice as that kiss was, I wasn't about to give up Barry!

The next day, Steve and I talked at work. He apologized for what had happened, but in my heart, I knew he wasn't sorry. He felt I belonged with him, not Barry, and he was quite vocal about that. The next day I told Barry what happened. I was so nervous telling him that

I stammered through the whole story. It was clear he was pissed off at Steve. Barry and Steve had been cool, but after the incident at Au Bon Pain, Barry never looked at Steve the same way, and they didn't have much to say to each other around the neighborhood anymore. I did continue my relationship with Barry, but not for long. Between my busy schedule and the guilt I felt over the kiss from Steve, I broke it off. To be honest, I didn't feel worthy of a relationship with Barry. I couldn't understand what he saw in a troubled girl like me. I had a messed-up family and lived in a group home. I also worried that I couldn't spend a lot of time with him. And even though he never pressured me about sex, I felt bad that we weren't sharing that experience.

As far as I was concerned, my past made me damaged goods, but I couldn't say that to Barry or anyone else for that matter. I was still too ashamed and embarrassed about what had happened to discuss it with anyone. I didn't think people would believe or respect me if they knew. I was certain they would think I was dirty because my own brother and cousin had touched me. I didn't realize that the same thing happened to other kids, and I sure as hell didn't know it had a name. It was incest.

Breaking up with Barry was one of the hardest things I ever had to do, and I deeply regretted every minute of it. I couldn't stop thinking about him even afterwards. A few weeks later, he began dating a girl named Sandra from school that I was cool with also. I was livid.

Even though she and I were just acquaintances, I felt betrayed. How could she date him? And how could he get with someone so soon after our breakup? I started giving them both the cold shoulder. I was uncomfortable being around Barry so I decided to ignore him. This was my petty, juvenile way of getting back at him for dating Sandra. Truthfully, I was mad at myself for giving up our relationship, but it was easier to be mad at them than to accept responsibility for my own actions. In spite of my childish behavior, Barry still remained nice to me. He even gave me a card for Christmas that year.

At the group home, things were actually getting better with my therapies, and I started to enjoy the Tuesday group sessions run by the program director, Buddy. Buddy was super cool — always very personable and extremely insightful. He was like a human lie detector. Buddy had an uncanny ability to unearth the truth from us kids. Thankfully, he never had to use his detective skills on me. He and I got along great, but I was still struggling in my family therapy sessions with Mom and Kate. I gave Kate a hard time, and I still resented my mom for believing my uncle's girlfriend over me. It was around this time that Mom told me she and Vance were expecting a baby. I had only met Vance a few times and didn't know much about him, but I was astonished she had let herself get pregnant by a man she had only known for a few months. There wasn't anything I could do about it, though, since she was already pregnant.

Meanwhile, my 18th birthday was fast approaching. I had not been a practicing Jehovah's Witness for nearly two years and had never celebrated a birthday before. The staff at Trinity knew this, and I told them not to do anything special, but on the Tuesday that preceded my birthday, they surprised me with a big chocolate cake before our group meeting. Finally, I understood why people felt so special on their birthday. For the next few days, I was on a birthday "high," but the feeling didn't last long. Shortly after my birthday, Rolanda called to tell me her mom passed away. She was only 45.

How could this be? I thought to myself. She was with me a couple of months ago, helping me find Bridge. I later found out she had been admitted to the hospital within days of taking me to Bridge and slipped into a diabetic coma a couple of weeks later. I couldn't believe that she spent her last few able-bodied days helping me find a home, despite her pain and weakness. For the next few days, I moped around Trinity and stayed holed up in my room crying. When I went back to Rolanda's house after the funeral, she and her mother's roommate asked me to move in. They insisted her mother would have wanted it that way. I knew they were right, but as flattered as I was, I politely declined. Her mother's death was a confirmation that I needed to get serious about Trinity and make it work. I did not want her death to be in vain.

Shortly after, Thanksgiving arrived. Kate thought it would be nice if I invited my mom to dinner, so I did. Surprisingly, everything went smoothly. After that, she and I began making more and more progress in our sessions with Kate. We even talked about the impact of Lisa's death. That conversation made me feel better because up to then, we had rarely mentioned Lisa's name. The more she discussed her feelings I became really receptive to her.

Christmas arrived pretty quickly too. I had mixed feelings about celebrating the holiday, but that all changed when I saw all the cool gifts that were donated to us. We received everything from new CD players to brand new coats! I was elated because I hadn't had any new clothes in years. My mother and I had shopped at Goodwill for so long that I barely remembered what new clothes looked like. I was now fully adjusted to living at Bridge. The people there were starting to be like the healthy family I never had.

Chapter 19

For the most part I was doing pretty well in school, but I was struggling with chemistry and math. Miraculously, I managed to pull my grade up to a C in chemistry, but I continued to receive Ds in algebra, so Trinity got me a tutor. His name was Sam Shapiro. Sam was a round Jewish accountant who volunteered once a week at Bridge as a math tutor. He took a special interest in me, and pretty soon my grades began to improve. I still struggled with math, but at least my homework was getting done.

Before Trinity, I had pretty much abandoned my dreams of going to college. But thanks to the great encouragement from the staff and Sam, that possibility began to seem more attainable. When I wasn't studying or working, I spent time down at the library. There, I obtained a college counselor named Nita Veselli. Nita was crazy cool. She gave me great advice about college, but I mostly enjoyed just going there to talk to her. I also spent a lot of time at the library pouring over college scholarship books and researching different colleges. Every week I mailed out applications and letters to different scholarship committees. Sam also was helping me prepare for the SAT.

Next thing I knew it, spring was upon us, and everything was starting to come to a head. There was the SAT, end-of-year testing, the prom and of course graduation. It was hard to believe I had made it this far! A few weeks before the prom, I received my first college response. After watching "A Different World" for many years, I was pretty hell-bent on going to a black college, so those were the only ones I applied to. The first letter I received was a rejection from Clark Atlanta University in Georgia. I was a little disappointed, but the staff encouraged me to stay hopeful. And they were right! A few weeks after receiving the Clark Atlanta rejection, I learned I was accepted into Virginia Union University (VUU) in Richmond.

I didn't know much about VUU. In fact, I hadn't even visited the school. I applied on the strength of its photogenic brochure. I was so excited to be accepted somewhere that I immediately confirmed my acceptance. With that out of the way, I focused on prom and graduation. I was happy the school year was winding down — it was awkward being in homeroom with Barry since I was still on my "I'm not speaking to you" strike. I guess it really troubled him, because a couple of days before the prom, he came to visit me at the group home, and we talked, hugged and wished each other well. I was glad that we were back on good terms. Despite my stubbornness, I really did miss Barry. Back then, he was the most charming guy I had ever met, and I still liked him as much as the day we had started going out.

With just a few days before the prom, I still didn't have a dress or a date. Thank God for my good friend Walt. As storybook as this may sound, he became my "fairy godfather," bringing me not one, but two dresses from the clothing store he worked at. Walt had impeccable taste, and both gowns were equally gorgeous. I spent the money Walt saved me on the dress on my hair. Back then, I wore a lot of hair weaves and considered myself an amateur "weavestress," gluing my own weaves onto my scalp. But for this occasion, I went to May's, a well-known Mattapan salon for the ghetto-fabulous.

I guess everyone else had the same idea, because the place was overflowing with other prom goers. The staff was clearly overwhelmed and ended up letting the perm sit on my hair a little too long. By the time they rinsed it out, I had blotches of open burns on my scalp. The pain was so intense it was hard to comb my hair. Combing, however, wasn't as painful as trying to glue the weave onto my scalp burns. Talk about ouch!!! Between all that hair drama and the waiting, I didn't get out of there until about an hour and half before prom.

I didn't have time to get my nails done, so I threw on some press-on nails. I also didn't have a date, so my good friend and housemate, Javier, agreed to go to the prom with me at the last minute. Javier was from Puerto Rico and had never been to a prom before, so he was just as excited as I was. The staff made a big production of the evening. They snapped pictures and made me feel like a queen for the day.

Buddy even participated, showing up in a tux and top hat to escort us to the prom in his BMW. Javier and I had so much fun dancing and "acting a fool" that I barely paid any attention to Barry and his girlfriend Sandra.

It was an exciting time of year for me! During the school awards ceremony, I received four small scholarships! And better yet, I received word that I had won the NAACP ACT-SO (Afro-Academic, Cultural, Technological and Scientific Olympics) regional competition in poetry. That meant I would compete in the nationals in Chicago! Although I didn't win the national competition, I met a lot of great people and received a $500 savings bond and free Reebok gear! Believe it or not, that trip almost didn't happen. When I was told I would have to fly to Chicago, I almost backed out! Watching me fly all over the place today, you would never know I was terrified back then.

My relationship with Mom had improved so much that she agreed to attend my graduation. It was there that my little sister, Sarah, just a couple of weeks old, made her debut. Trinity threw me a graduation party after the ceremony where I received many gifts, including a greeting card from Sam with $100 in it.

During the summer, I continued to work at Au Bon Pain and enrolled in another college-prep summer program. Trinity took some footage of me during the program for their first group-home documentary. Before I knew it, it was time to leave for college. Since schools down south started early, I left at the beginning of August. I knew I would miss my Bridge family, but I also knew I was more than ready to move on and become independent.

Chapter 20

The first thing I noticed about VUU was how small the school was. VUU's total enrollment, roughly 1,200 students, was almost that of my high school back in Massachusetts. I think I was more excited about being in college to really care at the time. Besides, I figured a smaller school meant smaller class sizes. That really appealed to me because I would get more personalized attention in my journalism classes.

When I arrived, there were long registration lines for everything, from dormitory assignments to class schedules. Exiting one of the administrative offices, I met two very tall, light-skinned ladies standing with a bunch of bags and boxes. One was the mother of a student, and the other was the student's grandmother. They were waiting for her return. I marveled at how much stuff she had. I ran into them again roaming the halls of the dorm. This time April, was with them. As it turned out, she lived right above me. April was a gregarious, liberal-minded, people-person from Queens, New York, and was crazy cool! We hit it off immediately.

Soon after, April introduced me to a vivacious girl named Micha, who came from Hampton, Virginia. Micha was an olive-complected girl with glasses. She was half black and part Native American. Her trademark was red lipstick with black liner and miniskirts with high heels. Consequently, she was an instant boy magnet. Though we had very different personalities, the three of us instantly bonded. Rarely would you see one of us without the other two.

In fact, hanging with them became my refuge to escape my messy roommate, Taneka. Taneka, a pretty caramel girl from Arlington, Virginia, was filthy in every sense of the word. She left clothes sprawled across her bed, which was never made, and bowls of food sitting for days on any available surface in the room. Judging by her nice clothes, you wouldn't think she was that dirty. Being a neat freak, I couldn't stand it. So, you can imagine how excited I was when she got a boyfriend and began spending her nights with him off campus.

Virginia Union was my own "A Different World." Just like the TV show, there were black fraternities and sororities, a Miss Black College Queen pageant, step show competitions and a marching band. Like the show, there also were unique students at VUU. One night, while my girls and I were out strolling the school grounds, we met a group of four guys: Truth, from Philly; Khalil and Tony, from New York; and Kevin, who we nicknamed "Tommy" after the "Martin" television character because he was so incognito. We hung out talking with them until our 10 p.m. curfew. From that point on, the seven of us were tight. When we weren't hanging with them, we were chilling with our friend, Sergio, our unofficial "chauffeur" for all off-campus parties. April, Micha and I were regulars on the party scene, so much so that people would call us to find out about upcoming parties.

Despite the partying, I earned my highest GPA ever during that year, a 3.6.

As the weeks went by, everyone started hooking up. Micha was dating several athletes on campus, and April was getting closer to Khalil. There were a couple of people who had crushes on me, but none really caught my attention seriously, that is, until I met Abry, a short, mocha-colored brother with a mustache. Abry was a couple of years older than me and did not go to VUU, but he frequented the campus. He belonged to a local R & B group that was trying to become the next Boyz II Men. Abry and I went out a few times, but we never materialized into a relationship.

When that possibility faded, I developed a crush on our friend, Truth, but it ended when he started dating Bette, a girl from my dorm. After that, I had my sights on Jones, a tan, muscular brother I only knew in passing. Unfortunately, I couldn't get him to pay attention to me. But I did get the attention of a new football player from California. Dennis, a short, dark-skinned jovial athlete, was nicknamed "11:59." His teammates joked that someone that dark had to be identified as a minute before midnight, thus the name. While I wasn't attracted to him romantically, we did become good friends. Back then, it wasn't the guys who didn't want relationships with me; I couldn't initiate a relationship. I still couldn't see myself being intimate with anyone. I didn't realize the past molestation was holding me back from developing meaningful relationships at VUU. As far as I was concerned, I was still damaged goods.

Micha's luck was much better than mine — or so I thought. She had men approaching her on and off campus, but she became so consumed with all of the attention that her grades began to suffer. I guess I really didn't know how bad things were, until I received a call one night from our friend, KaQuan, who we nicknamed "Shaq" because of his strong resemblance to the ballplayer.

"Sylvia, you better get over to the boy's dorm quick. These dudes are about to run a train on Micha," he said.

I got over to the basketball house just in time. Micha was drunk and stumbling all over the place. Fortunately I reached her before the guys could get her clothes off. I balanced her with my arms, and we made our way back to the girls' dorm, where she passed out across the bed.

****

Life at VUU wasn't all about boys. Being at a black college exposed me to a lot of my African-American history, and I started to become more culturally and politically conscious. Thus, I changed my appearance as I changed my views. Ever since my horrible hair accident right before the prom, I had started to sport braids. I also resumed writing poetry, which led to performing at spoken word venues. I even joined the campus newspaper, a community weekly, the student National Association of Black Journalists and Toastmasters. To this day, I'm not sure how I fit all that activity into my party and school schedule!

However, it was the after-effects of one party that caused me to slow down. Me, Shaq, April, Micha, Tony, our friend "Grandpa" and Rashawn had just left a party downtown. Rashawn was feeling down because his girl had broken up with him, so he separated from us to walk alone ahead of us. For whatever reason, he took a shortcut through an abandoned shopping lot where there were no street lamps. We didn't want anything bad to happen to him, so we followed him. Big mistake! No, a huge mistake! We were about halfway across the lot when we heard several loud pops. The next thing I knew, everyone had disbanded. Shaq was the first to leave and literally jumped over the hood of a parked car. April darted between vehicles in the adjacent lot. Oblivious to what was going on, Grandpa and I lingered.

"What's going on?" I shouted.

"Shots, Shots!" someone yelled.

As soon as I heard that, I grabbed Grandpa's arm, and we jetted out of that dark alley. By the time we caught up with the rest of the crew, they were halfway down the next street, doubled over in laughter at how slow we were. I just thank God we all made it out of there unharmed. However, I couldn't help but wonder how Shaq got his big body over that car so fast! From then on, we did most of our partying on campus.

As the school year moved on, we saw the campus go downhill academically and physically. Apparently VUU was having administrative and funding problems. April and I got fed up and started searching for another school. That's when we visited Howard University, another popular black college in Washington, D.C. We actually went to attend a communications job fair, but made a point to check out the campus while there. Impressed by what we saw, we were convinced it was time to move on from VUU.

We both wanted to stay at a black school, but April couldn't afford Howard's expensive tuition, so she applied to Morgan State University in Baltimore. I applied to Howard in hopes of getting a good financial aid package, but searched for a back-up school in case things fell through with Howard. April suggested Temple University in Philadelphia, since it had a large black population. After visiting the campus, I applied to there as well and decided I would go with the first school to respond.

Chapter 21

Though we were sad about leaving our VUU friends, we knew we were better off going while we still could. Micha knew this, too and opted not to return to college after our freshman year.

Halfway through the summer, Temple accepted me, and April was accepted into Morgan State. I didn't hear from Howard until the end of the summer. Although they accepted me, it was too late to secure housing and financial aid for that school year. Temple, on the other hand, had set me up with a single room on its health science campus. Each resident in that dorm had their own room, and since we didn't have an on-site cafeteria like the other dormitories, we had special meal privileges at Temple University Hospital. The food at the hospital, which was adjacent to our dorm, was 10 times better than the food on main campus! We also had student access to Temple's Health Sciences' fitness center and a state-of-the-art computer lab, both right across the street. If we wanted to get to main campus, all we had to do was call for the free campus shuttle. Although the health sciences campus was nice, I spent a lot of time at the main campus because that's where all my classes were. Plus, I had landed a work study job in the school of communications there.

Porcha Peterson was the first person I met when I took my tour of the campus over the summer. She was an executive member of the African Student Union (ASU), but had left the organization by the time I arrived in September of 1995. I ran into her again at the main campus, and we instantly clicked. In fact, we are still good friends today.

Hearing her talk about the progressive agenda of the ASU, I was compelled to join. I worked under Vincent Jones on the advertising committee. Also in the organization were Niesha, Nelson and Brother Juru. Through them, I met other former ASU members, like Candace, our advisor, and Jerome. Jerome was a smooth, tan brother with long [dread] locs. I was instantly attracted to him. He was working on his Masters in Education through Temple's graduate program, and was a regular participant in many of the black organizations on campus like the Organization of African Students (OAS), the Student Organization of Caribbean Students (SOCA) and the Haitian Student Organization (HSO).

Because all these organizations were housed in the same building, I ran into Jerome quite a bit. Eventually, he asked me out, and we began spending more and more time together. Jerome was quite adventurous. He loved everything from skydiving to horseback riding, and he introduced me to several exceptional eateries around town. Eventually, our relationship became more intimate. With Jerome, I felt very comfortable and uninhibited. It was the first time I felt comfortable enough to be intimate with someone since that awful encounter with my cousin down south. As time went on, my feelings for Jerome grew stronger. I was completely infatuated with this man. We definitely enjoyed each other's company, but Jerome said he wasn't ready for a boyfriend/girlfriend relationship. He could see my apprehension about that, so he reassured me our relationship was exclusive. We went on like this for about five or six months.

By this time I had made a lot of friends on campus, becoming especially close to my good friend, Gerard, whom I started calling my little brother. Gerard's sisters, Vanessa and Kelly, also went to Temple, and I was cool with them as well. Gerard knew I was spending time with somebody, and kept asking who I was dating. I was used to his impromptu interrogations and managed to avoid answering him for quite some time. I'm not sure what compelled me, but one day I broke down and told him it was Jerome.

"Jerome with the long locs?" he asked in disbelief.

"Yeah! Why do you ask?"

"I don't know if I should tell you this…" he started.

"Tell me what, Gerard?" I demanded. "Spit it out!"

"Jerome's seeing Ashante."

Ashante? I thought to myself. Not the same Ashante I knew! I felt like the bottom of my stomach was about to drop out of my body.

"You're kidding me!" I finally responded. "Are you sure?" I was obviously in denial. Deep in my heart, however, I knew Gerard was telling the truth; I just didn't want to hear it. I stormed away. He tried to calm me down, but all I could think about was confronting Jerome. I ran into him on the stairway to the ASU office. I can't remember what I said, but I know he tried to grab my arm. I yanked myself free and sprinted down the stairs. Later on that evening, I caught up with him again in front of the library. "What's this I hear about you and Ashante?" Just as we were about to get into it, she rounded the corner.

I stopped her. "Ashante, are you seeing Jerome?"

Jerome intervened. He had no choice but to confess. It turned out he had been with her for almost as long as he had been seeing me. I wanted to clock the bastard in the face. Instead, I left the two of them standing there. Jerome begged me to come back, but I hopped on the shuttle bus and went back to my dorm. When I got back to my room, the phone started ringing. I answered.

"I can explain. Can I come up?" he pleaded, but I hung up on him. He kept calling, and each time, I hung up. After a while, he started bugging the security guard to let him see me. I guess she grew tired of his pleas, because she told me to come down and "take care of him." Reluctantly, I went. Jerome was sitting in the common room by himself. The more he talked, the more he kept putting his foot in his mouth.

"That's it," I said interrupting him. "I've had enough. I'm going back to my room."

Then he really got melodramatic! Jerome fell to his knees, locked his arms around my waist, and started sobbing and imploring me to give him another chance. The begging went on for a good few minutes before I managed to free myself and walk away.

Though Jerome continued to call, I just let the phone ring. Eventually he got the message, because he stopped calling. I guess he decided to try his begging act on Ashante, because a few days later I saw them getting out of his car, looking extremely happy. What a traitor! I thought. How could she be so stupid? He played both of us! From that day on, I ceased all communication with the both of them, but I was still not over Jerome. I really still liked him and couldn't believe how he betrayed the trust I had waited so long to have with a guy. The situation made me feel like damaged goods and once again like a sexual victim.

****

The next few months were very depressing ones for me. I could barely stand the sight of Ashante and Jerome and so avoided going any place I thought they would be. To deal with the upset, I increased my workload. I took on another job at Hats in the Belfry on South Street and an internship at MetroKids magazine. I also took on the advertising chair position for the ASU. Talk about busy!

Around this same time, I won a scholarship from the Professional Golf Writer's Schripp Association. They flew all of the winners out to

Louisville, Kentucky, to receive the prize. While there, we toured the PGA tournament, where we got to see Muhammad Ali and Tiger Woods on the golf course. "Tiger who?" I said to the staff. Back then, I had no idea who he was, so I opted out of meeting him. Ignorant, huh?

It was hard to move on from Jerome, but I definitely tried. I soon developed a crush on my good friend, Kenneth, who like me was from Massachusetts. Kenneth was a funny, sarcastic brother who looked a lot like the singer Seal. He was also a huge Mary J. Blige fan and had a life-size door-length poster of her in his dorm room to prove it. I tried to drop Kenneth several hints that I was interested, but he did not reciprocate. Why isn't he interested in me? I thought. Maybe he was into light-skinned girls. But I was wrong. Two years later, a mutual friend informed me Kenneth was gay. He said when he confronted him about it, Kenneth stopped speaking to him. To this day Kenneth and I have never openly discussed his sexuality.

Meanwhile, my best friend April was doing great at Morgan State. Micha had moved to Baltimore too and landed a job stripping in a nude bar. That really concerned us because Micha was a magnet for trouble. Since she was our girl, we didn't want to judge her for her decision, so we just told her to be careful. I guess Micha felt ashamed about her lifestyle, because not too long after that, she disappeared. From time to time, we would hear from friends that she was still dancing, but we had no way to contact her.

Chapter 22

My busy schedule began to cause my grades to slip. Fortunately, a wonderful professor had the good sense to remind me to get back on track in time for graduation.

Reluctantly, I limited my time with the ASU, finished up my internship and quit my work study job. Cutting back on my time with the ASU was the hardest, since the executive committee had become like family to me. However, with the addition of Tito, the organization's first Puerto Rican member and our newest executive board member, I felt a little better about moving on. Tito was like a big brother to me and reassured me that I was doing the right thing. Almost immediately, I began to reap the benefits of that difficult decision. My grades significantly improved, and the school of communications renewed my PGW scholarship.

Meanwhile, I took on more responsibility at the hat store. The manager went on maternity leave, so I became acting manager. Two months later, I resumed my role as assistant manager. Everyone who worked there was crazy cool, including the manager. We'd sit around and chill, meeting all kinds of fun people. In fact, I met many of my friends first as customers at the store. I guess I got a little too comfortable there because the owner's daughter came in one day and spotted me sitting down on the job. She reported the incident to her father, and they promptly fired me.

I was shocked. I had been there for two-and-a-half years and had hoped to finish out my senior year there. What was I going to do? I had just rented a new apartment down the street from my job and did not know how I would pay the $425 rent. To make matters worse, I quickly ran out of food. Depression set in, and I began to worry day and night about the bills. What would I do? Where would I get money? They say you really know who your friends are when times get rough. Sometimes it's the person you least expect who steps up to the plate. My friend Sean, a short, humorous brother from West Philly, was this friend for me. He strongly believed in helping his fellow brothers and sisters.

It was 1998, and I had met Sean earlier that summer, so I had only known him for a couple of months. Even though I was very attracted to him, our friendship never materialized into anything more. Still, Sean always had my back, and this time, he really came through. When he found out I lost my job, he promptly brought over some delicious Caribbean cuisine from down the street. Sensing that was not enough, he took me grocery shopping that same week. I thought I would just get a few boxes of macaroni and call it a day, but Sean wouldn't hear of it. When we left the store, we had five bags of groceries that were bursting at the seams! And, to top that off, Sean paid my rent! I was overwhelmed by his kindness. I promised to give the money back to him, but he declined the repayment. Till this day, he remains a good and faithful friend.

Somehow I sensed a new beginning, a change coming in my life. I had been contemplating locing my hair for the last few years, but did not have the guts. Sensing that apprehension, my best friend April sat me down and started locing my hair before I had a chance to refuse. It was definitely a big change for me! With my short, sassy locs, I felt ready to step back into the world and get noticed again. After a brief stint in telemarketing, I landed a job at one of the nation's oldest black newspapers. Ironically, the office was just two blocks from where I lived. The pay was $21,000 — not much, but still a blessing.

Chapter 23

When I arrived at my new job, there were only four women working in the editorial department: Lydia, Karen, Sharon and Tabitha. I initially thought I would be placed in the same room with them, but the managing editor opted to seat me in the main newsroom with all the men. There I quickly learned that no subject was off limits. In fact, we often joked that the material was raw enough for an HBO sitcom.

In the main newsroom with me were Bernard, a shameless flirt who knew the who's who of Philadelphia; Ned, a liberal general assignment reporter; Tad, our sarcastic education reporter from the suburbs; Glenda, a tall, light-skinned sister who served as secretary; Ted, an older white man with a distinct funny odor; Remy, a tall, brown-skinned fellow who was in the process of leaving the company; Manny, our culturally conscious political reporter; Mitchell, my effeminate boss from Indiana; Ken, a thin political reporter who loved to eat; and Maurice, a tall, light-skinned, cocky flirt.

I was put in charge of the Philadelphia and New Jersey educational supplements for kids in grades K-12. I didn't have a car, so getting around to the different schools was very challenging. Some days I was lucky enough to hitch a ride with a staff photographer. Most of the time, however, I was on my own. I didn't know it then, but I should have been getting paid more for the amount of work I was doing putting together two educational supplements. Since I was a staff of just one, I often struggled to meet weekly deadlines. Fortunately, they sent an intern my way. Her typing skills came in handy when I needed some transcribing.

Meanwhile, I became very close to Lydia, Tad and Manny. When we could, Lydia and I would go to my place for our one-hour lunch break and watch "The Young and the Restless." If I was really tired, I'd come home alone and take a nap during lunch. Most lunch hours, however, I would go out with my co-workers, Tad and Manny, and eat at Pinky's down the street. Pinky's, famous for its pastries, served breakfast and lunch all day, so we were instantly hooked.

Like I said, the newspaper had a couple of well-known flirts, but I wasn't too keen on mixing business with pleasure, especially since the incident during high school at Au Bon Pain with my co-worker. Nothing good could come out of it, I surmised. However, when Remy left the newspaper he asked me out on a date. I hadn't dated in a while, so I went for it. Although Remy and I had a pleasant evening, our date never materialized into anything more. Meanwhile, Maurice, who already had a girlfriend down South, tried to make moves on me, saying stuff like, "I like that skirt on you," as his eyes lingered on my rear. I didn't take him seriously. He seemed like the type who would date several women at once. In fact, I recall telling my co-worker Tad I'd be stupid to go out with him because he was sure to play me.

Besides, Maurice had a very sharp tongue and wasn't afraid to use it. He could compliment and insult you in the same breath and wouldn't apologize. He was also known for his arrogant ramblings where he would declare himself the best reporter at the newspaper. Most of the time, however, Maurice was very funny. He always had an entertaining story or lewd joke to share. Sometimes though, you couldn't tell if he was joking or serious because of his poker face. In any case, you didn't want to find out because Maurice's temper could go from zero to 60 in three minutes. In spite of this flaw, some found him charming, while others thought he was a bona-fide jerk. Either way, you couldn't tune him out because Maurice's personality was larger than life, and he had an uncanny way of leaving an indelible impression on everyone who met him.

As the weeks went by, I continued to ignore his advances. Regardless of how subtle they were, Maurice never made a direct move. The flirting went on for nearly three months. Christmas rolled around and we were getting the next couple of days off. On our last day in the office, Ted and Maurice were sitting in the newsroom alone, finishing up last-minute work. Most everybody had left the newsroom to start their holiday early, but I was coming back late from an assignment. When I entered, Jack and Maurice were discussing about their holiday plans. I caught just enough to hear that Maurice wasn't doing anything special. Anxious to get out of there, I sat down and began packing my briefcase.

"Sylvia, what are you doing for the holidays?" Ted blurted out.

"Nothing," I responded.

"Nothing?" he queried. "Since neither of you have any plans, why don't you do nothing together?"

I admit I was a little taken aback by Ted's forwardness, but he did have a point, so Maurice and I agreed to exchange numbers.

Besides, I viewed Maurice as just a co-worker like my good friends, Tad and Manny, so it would be just platonic socializing. I also didn't think a ladies' man like Maurice would be calling me anytime soon. So I gave him my number and forgot all about it. The next day, a Saturday, I didn't have anything special planned, so I decided to do my hair. By this time, my locs were down to my ear, and it took me two hours to wash, condition and re-twist them. I was halfway through the process when the phone rang. It was none other than Maurice. I gasped.

"I didn't expect to hear from you," I blurted out.

He asked if I wanted to hang out.

"Sure!" I said, touching my unfinished hair. I figured what the hell — if anything, Maurice would not be boring. I quickly hopped into some fitted jeans and tied my hair up in an Erykah Badu-style gele. Not bad for short notice, I thought. Maurice arrived 30 minutes later, looking impeccably hot! I had never seen him outside of work and dressed casually, so I was impressed by his loose designer jeans, leather jacket and the skully cap he had so casually cocked to the side of his head.

That night, we went to Wilamina's, one of the hottest, underground retro-soul venues in the city. There weren't a lot of people there, so it was easy to find a secluded, cozy booth in the rear of the lounge. Maurice ordered our drinks. I had a large Long Island ice tea. Almost immediately, I started feeling more relaxed, and Maurice sensed it. Perhaps it was the drink, but everything he said to me sounded seductive. Looking into his chestnut eyes, I was definitely starting to "feel this brother." Believe it or not, as flirtatious as we were in that booth, we did manage to have an intelligent conversation. We talked about everything from politics to black folks to relationships. Back then, I didn't think a pretty boy could be that intelligent, but there was something intriguing about Maurice. He could pull a stat out of his head like he was a human encyclopedia.

We stayed at Wilamina's for an hour and a half before we decided to get out of there. We were both having a really good time, so we decided to keep hanging out. I wasn't sure where else to go, so he asked if I wanted to hang at his house. I agreed, not knowing he lived way out in the 'burbs.' We drove to a town called Blue Bell, which I had never heard of before. Then we drove into a gated community of huge homes that looked like something out of Better Homes & Gardens magazine

I started to panic. Where is this man taking me? We could get in trouble hanging in a white neighborhood like this. They'll probably call the cops on us, I thought to myself. Talk about ignorant! It never occurred to me that Maurice lived on this beautiful, one-acre property until we drove up to a gorgeous home made of stucco.

"Here we are!" he announced.

"You live here?"

"Yeah!" he replied. "Let me show you around."

****

His family was away in Louisiana for the holidays, so the place was empty. The house had everything: A vast TV room, with ceiling-high plants and sliding glass doors that opened to the backyard terrace; a lovely breakfast nook in the kitchen; an adjoining dining room that trailed out to a patio; and an adjacent, stylish living room, replete with a series of elegantly-framed family photos. Then we toured upstairs, where Maurice showed me the four bedrooms, including his parents' bedroom, which had its own Jacuzzi.

Back downstairs, he took out some liquor, and we played a sort of truth or dare game. Of course, he had some dirty dares for me. If I wasn't chugging down a shot, he was challenging me to an intimate dare. Hence, our first kiss. I think we must have re-invented kissing that night! It didn't take long for me to get real tipsy. In fact, I got downright drunk. Unable to drink anymore, I plopped onto the couch, where we continued making out. Things got hot and heavy, but fortunately I had the good sense to stop before we went too far.

The next thing I knew, it was morning and Maurice was nudging me to get up. Apparently his family had come home earlier than expected from Louisiana, and they were unpacking their car in the driveway. I was looking a mess and didn't want to meet them in that condition so I pulled the covers over my head and pretended to be asleep. Fortunately, they headed straight upstairs. I don't know what he told them about who I was, but he had them come into the house quietly so they wouldn't "wake" me.

Once they were all upstairs, I got myself together, and we headed out. While trying to leave, we ran into Maurice's father, also named Maurice. I was in awe of how much they looked alike. Maurice's father, a gregarious man, came over and gave me a big bear hug. As I've said, Maurice had a sick sense of humor, so on the drive home, he teased me, saying I was "grinding on his Pops." No, it was not your conventional date, but we both knew that the sparks were beginning to fly. "I really like this girl," he told his sister later that evening after taking me home. "There's something special about her."

Chapter 24

By this point, my mother and I had become a lot closer. Since our therapy at Bridge, we talked every week, always ending our calls with "I love you," something we never did before. As my relationships with my mom and Maurice began to grow, my mother's relationship with her fiancé, my little sister's father, began to fall apart.

Although I had only met one of Vance's children, apparently he had many others. My mother announced that Vance's daughter from Norwood was coming to visit with her own baby.

"Norwood?" I asked. There weren't many minorities in Norwood at the time, so my curiosity was definitely piqued. I wondered if I knew her.

"What's her name?" I asked my mom.

"Her name is Glenda."

"Glenda? Glenda?" I repeated to myself.

"You're not talking about Glenda Perez, are you? The same Glenda who has a younger brother Sean?"

"Yes," my mother responded. "They're Vance's son and daughter."

I was utterly flabbergasted. Glenda and I had both dated John in high school, and as a result never became friends. Her brother, on the other hand, I was cool with. I couldn't believe the indirect way we were now related. What a small world! And boy, did Vance get around! Little did we know then how much.

Not too long after the visit, Vance began working on ships overseas. When he came back some months later, he moved back in with his mom, or so we thought. One day, my little sister, then about four or five, was going on about how she had seen and played with a woman's pretty little baby at Daddy's house.

"What baby? What house?" my mother asked. Of course, being a toddler, my little sister didn't have all of the details, but she told my mother she could show her how to get to Daddy's house if she wanted to see the baby. My little sister was practically raised on public transportation and knew her way quite well around the city, so she was able to show Mom which buses to take to get there. When they arrived, my mother was taken aback. Vance had not been living with his mother at all; he had been shacking up with a young Latina who had just given birth to his baby. That was the end of Mom's engagement. Since that day, she and my sister have never seen Vance again.

My mother was very upset that night. When we spoke on the phone, she sounded dejected. I had rarely seen her that way. The only good thing about the situation was that she had finally seen Vance's true character. He had concocted a whole web of lies about everything from his fidelity to having custody of one of his son. My mother's friends and I always felt there was something shady about Vance, and this melee had confirmed just how deceitful he was. I was relieved she finally saw him for who he really was.

While Mom was dealing with her personal crisis, I was busy trying to figure Maurice out. A few weeks after our initial date, we finally became intimate. I guess I was really starting to fall for him, because being with him intimately felt very right. I didn't feel awkward or shameful as I had in previous relationships. Things felt very natural. Maurice was a lot of fun and very spontaneous. One day, he would whisk me off to Atlantic City for the weekend; the next, he would be in my kitchen showing off his cooking skills as he did our first Valentine's Day together when he cooked linguini and clams sautéed in wine. Maurice definitely knew how to romance a woman, but just like my former flame, Jerome, he could not commit. No one knew about our relationship at work.

On the job, we were in heavy negotiations with the union over our contracts. Because I lived closest to the newspaper, it was easier to have the meetings at my house. Everyone, including Maurice, would come over for the meetings. When they were over, Maurice would be first to leave, but he'd drive back about a half hour later after everyone was gone and we would go out together. We laughed at how we had them all fooled. Initially, Maurice and I wanted to keep it that way, because we knew the newspaper was "gossip central," and also because secrecy made our rendezvous fun. However, it didn't take long for my friend Clarise to figure it out. We suspected a few more people knew, but were simply too scared to confront us about it. No one wanted to incur Maurice's wrath or risk being embarrassed by him.

After a couple of months, however, it became evident that our relationship was getting more serious. We were spending significantly more time together. Sneaking around was no longer exciting. I wanted a commitment from Maurice, but he refused, questioning my intentions. I explained to him I did not want a repeat of the horrible experience I had with Jerome. Every few days I'd nag Maurice about a commitment, but we just ended up going around in circles and getting angry.

He claimed he didn't want to be in a relationship unless the woman was in love with him. This was one of our biggest issues because Maurice had actually professed his love for me almost two months into the relationship. As flattered as I was by his declaration, I just wasn't ready to repeat it back to him. I knew it was a major step for Maurice to disclose his feelings, but he had completely caught me off guard. Truth be told, I had nothing to base *real* love on, and had too much fear from my past to pronounce my love for *anyone*. However, I did let him know that I had never been more receptive toward falling in love with someone than I was with him.

Besides the commitment issue, there were other issues that were starting to concern me about Maurice — things I had tried desperately to ignore since our first date. Maurice was an excessive drinker and would often leave in the middle of the night to buy liquor. Or, he'd get so inebriated he'd pass out before we had a chance to go anywhere. Also, his mood would fluctuate like the seasons. One minute he was really happy and acting silly; the next, he was giving me the cold shoulder.

The other thing that concerned me was his refusal to wear a condom. This choice, I admit, was as much his fault as mine. A couple of times I was able to persuade him to wear one, but we were too far gone in this reckless habit to commit to change. People who know me, know this is not the type of thing I would normally do, especially considering how adamant I now am about safe sex. The truth is I allowed myself to change during the course of the relationship because I did not have a clue about who I was. Like my previous relationships, I could not distinguish right from wrong. I didn't know it then, but my inability to practice sound judgment and healthy boundaries stemmed from the molestation I had endured in the past — beginning long before Maurice entered my life. Despite the fact that I showed all the signs of a sexual abuse survivor (poor concentration, perfectionism, depression and detachment from friends and loved ones), I was still in denial about the impact the abuse had had on my life. As far as I was concerned, it was everyone else's fault my life was such a mess.

Feeling that Maurice was the problem, I broke things off in early April. It was easier to blame him than look at my own issues. He didn't react in a mean way to my decision. In fact, he said he hoped I would continue to speak to him at work. Well, that break-up didn't last long. By the first evening, we were back together. He called me to tell me about some drama he had going on with his father and said he needed to get out of the house. I let him come over, and we resumed our relationship. "I knew you still liked me by the way you smiled and wouldn't let go of my hand," Maurice said of our earlier departure. It was true.

Still, his drinking did not cease. In fact, he escalated to asking me for money to buy his liquor. Initially, I had no idea he was spending the cash I gave him on alcohol, because he would just ask to borrow a few dollars until the next day. Naïve, wasn't I! By the time I figured out what he was really doing with the money, I had become a full-fledged enabler. By the end of April, just four months into our renewed relationship, we broke up again, but this time it was ugly. I broke up with him through a letter. It wasn't a nasty letter but, nonetheless, it was an impersonal way to go. That letter didn't go over too well with Maurice. He gave me the cold shoulder when I asked how he felt about it. Despite this initial reaction, Maurice continued to be cordial, speaking to me when he saw me and even giving me a ride home one evening. Despite our many issues, that was one thing I could say about Maurice: he'd help you out even if the two of you weren't on good terms.

As challenging as our relationship sometimes was, it was even harder for us to be apart. Maurice and I had an unusually strong connection for such a short relationship. We were uniquely intuitive to each other's needs. He was a keen listener, even when I could or would not disclose my thoughts. As if reading my mind, he would rattle off whatever I was thinking, virtually verbatim. It was like this even during our break-ups. Knowing each other that well was a blessing and a curse. During our break-ups we resorted to petty behavior to gnaw on each other's nerves — I wouldn't speak to him at work (which really pissed him off), and he would attempt to make me jealous by sharing stories of different female conquests of his with our co-workers — very juvenile behavior indeed.

That year, 1999, we got back together and broke up at least two more times. The break-ups were always initiated by me, and he'd always call to get us back together. On the surface, this roller coaster was always over the same issues: lack of commitment, whether or not to go public with our relationship and, of course, his excessive drinking. The real issues, however, were yet to be exposed.

Chapter 25

By this time, I was already well acquainted with Maurice's family, especially his older sister, Trina. She and I had become especially close. Trina was extremely pleasant and in many ways reminded me of my own deceased sister, Lisa.

I didn't realize it then, but I had tried to fill Lisa's shoes with many female friends over the years: Melody, Stacey, Andrea, April and now Maurice's sister, Trina. Trina and I liked each other so much that we began spending more and more time together and often talked on the phone. We frequented concerts, plays and movies. I tried to get Maurice to go to these same places, but he would decline, saying he wasn't much for crowds or simply felt too sick to go (usually from drinking).

I also got along well with Maurice's teenage sister, Theresa. We'd act silly around the house, laughing and watching the latest music videos. Even his little nephew, Jeffrey, whom Maurice was particularly close to, adored me. That little boy would smooch and embrace me every chance that he got. I became close to Maurice's parents as well. If I stayed overnight, his mother and I were usually the first to rise in the morning. We'd sit in the kitchen, chatting away about everything from life and politics to work and Maurice. She was easy to talk to, and so was his father, who insisted I call him "Pop."

Initially Maurice was very excited about this rapport. He loved the fact that I got along so well with his family, but later he became jealous. He started saying stuff like, "You love my family more than me," and "They're the only reason why you come over to the house." It took a while to get Maurice to stop tripping over this nonsense. Although he ceased ranting about the issue, I don't think he completely put the accusation out of his mind. In time, I began to see that was how Maurice expressed himself whenever he was insecure. He'd get jealous and swear I was seeing someone else or complain that I was spending too much time with his family.

The irony was that he could be just as loving as he could be jealous or angry. He was extremely sincere and wouldn't say or do anything he didn't mean, so when he said, "I love you," he was seriously genuine. He was always saying very complimentary things like, "I love your hair," "You're the smartest woman I know," or "You look sexy in that dress." As I mentioned before, Maurice gave great advice and was a walking, talking encyclopedia of random knowledge. In our relationship, he did all the cooking. He'd drive me to doctor's appointments, the supermarket and other places — patiently wait for me to finish whatever I needed to do.

In fact, during the first year, Maurice asked me to marry him saying he'd like to start a family. I laughed it off because I thought he was joking; plus he had asked me right after sex. Maurice had a very dry sense of humor, so I thought this was another one of his silly jokes but, he was quite serious and seemed a little offended by my cavalier response. Deep inside, however, I knew we weren't ready for marriage. I was, by this point, very much in love with Maurice, but we both had too many issues. I had already filled up two journals, detailing my erratic relationship with Maurice and whether or not to leave.

In the fall of 1999, Maurice was diagnosed with an ulcer and severe anxiety attacks, no doubt due to his drinking. His health continued to decline, forcing him to frequently leave work early or call out for the day. Sometimes I'd take the day off to take care of him. By this point, I was spending little time with friends and family. Much of my free time was spent taking care of Maurice. "You bring out the best in me," he confessed to me one evening. "But, I'm scared of you...How do I know you're not going to abandon me anymore?" It was clear Maurice needed me now more than ever.

My friends tried to intervene, but I pushed them away, not wanting them to sway me from my decision. My old friend, Tito, told me I should move on. Insulted, I ended our friendship. The truth is, I couldn't stand hearing the truth. One night, I told Melody what was going on and she too expressed concern, "Is it worth it?" she asked. "I think so." The words slipped out before I could take them back. I was confused, drained and depressed, but did not have the courage to confess those feelings to any of my friends. I didn't want them to judge Maurice or scrutinize my decision to stay with him. Maurice was my first love, and I was too terrified of losing him. The only place I could be candid with myself was in my journal, where I unfurled all of my shame, unedited.

****

On January 15, 2000, things came to a head. Maurice was driving home from work around 2 p.m. when his eyesight began to dim. Feeling he would lose control of his car, he immediately threw the gears into park, or so he thought. His eyesight was so blurry that he shifted the car into reverse, hitting the vehicle directly behind him. By this time, he had completely passed out. He was pulled out of the car and rushed to the hospital, where they ran a battery of tests that included X-rays and a complete work-up of his blood, including an HIV test (which, thank God, came back negative). When he regained consciousness, he filled me in on what happened, but nothing prepared me for his next words:

"It turns out I have liver disease." His voice was audibly trembling. "I'm in the early stages of liver disease." For the next few seconds we were both silent. I was in a state of complete bewilderment, as if I had heard him incorrectly.

"What does that mean?" I asked.

"It means I can't drink anymore," he said sarcastically.

I knew he drank a lot, but damn! There was no denying it now. Evidently his family didn't know he drank so much either because his father was equally stunned.

"Boy, you mean to tell me you drank that much?" his father said at the hospital. "Is that what you were doing all that time you spent alone in your room? What were you drinking up there?" he asked.

"Mostly whiskey," Maurice responded.

"You're kidding," I said, still in disbelief, but this diagnosis was no joke. Maurice's sister later told me that they found a whole slew of empty liquor bottles under his bed. The doctor said he suffered a grand mal seizure in his car. I didn't need to ask what that was, because my mother had suffered one when I was 15. Apparently Maurice's seizure was caused by alcohol withdrawal. The doctor warned him that he'd probably have another one as he continued to detox.

Now, more than ever, I saw he needed my support, so I put the problems in our relationship on the back burner once again. The next day, I spent hours at a bookstore pouring over every bit of information I could find on liver disease. I ended up buying a natural healing book that outlined the benefits of milk thistle, a plant-based herb that works to heal the liver. I had been so dogged about Maurice's care that I practically ignored my own health. My weight was fluctuating, and I kept having sporadic periods and severe cramping. Fearing I was pregnant, I ran out and bought a test. Thank God it was negative!

With Maurice's severe health problems, it would be the worst timing to have a baby.

Detox was arduous for Maurice. His anxiety kicked in big time. He seemed to always have such a frightened look in his eyes, as if someone had stolen his joy. He tried to use humor to cope, but I could see the fear imbedded in his eyes.

"I have two years to live," he blurted out one day. I got very quiet. Sensing my apprehension, he tried to clean up the confession, "Just kidding," he said, interrupting my solemn thoughts. I didn't push the subject, but I also didn't believe his poor attempt to change the topic. Ironically, his pain caused me to reflect on my own life. For the first time in years, I started to consciously recall the sexual abuse. The secrecy of our relationship made me think of the secrecy surrounding the molestation, like a dirty little secret. I tried to suppress the thoughts from my mind when Maurice reassured me he loved me, but I couldn't help but wonder where we were really headed.

"I love you. There is no doubt in my mind," he said.

Unable to handle the symptoms of withdrawal, Maurice went back to drinking less than two months after his accident. "Before, I drank because I wanted to. Now, I don't want to. I don't even desire the taste for it, but I can't quit," he confessed. "I can't put it down."

On top of the drinking, he was still taking anxiety medicine and the milk thistle I gave him, which made me feel both relived and concerned, because I knew it was a bad combination. Worried, I called one of the alcohol cessation hotlines. A woman answered and explained that in Maurice's case he would not be able to detox on his own because of how far along his addiction was.

"Detoxing could take anywhere from three to 10 days, depending on the person, and he would have to admit himself to a facility. Alcohol is the hardest substance to detox from because of the seizures people suffer from during the process," she said. She told me he would not be able to do much of anything on his own, including pee.

"He's going to shake from the tremors…It will be painful," she added, "But the volume medication can treat the seizures."

She also told me something I already knew, but didn't have the guts to admit aloud.

"You're enabling him," she said. "You can't save him. He has to want it for himself." She encouraged me to go to Al-Anon, an organization for family and friends of alcoholics.

"And," she paused.

"And what?" I asked, sensing the hesitation in her voice.

"If he relapses," she continued. "You should leave him and let his family be his support system."

Stunned by her candor, I could barely hold the phone to my ear. This advice was especially bothersome for me to hear, and the hotline worker knew it. I tried to stifle my tears, but she could hear me sniffling through the phone.

"Are you okay?"

"I will be," I finally managed to say.

"I know," she said. "It's just a little close to home for you … I'll say a prayer for you."

When I got off the phone, I prayed like I never prayed before for what seemed like an hour. I asked God to do whatever He needed to do to heal Maurice, even if He had to take me out of his life.

It seemed like everything else was falling apart too. My mother had another grand mal seizure, which caused her to fall out of bed. I thought that was odd, since she hadn't had a seizure since we lived down south years ago. But then again, she had stopped taking her seizure medicine years ago, because she didn't like the way it made her feel.

My little sister, then just five, had no idea what was going on, but thank God she had enough sense to call 911. When they arrived, however, Sarah was still in shock and was too afraid to let them in. My mother had trained her not to open the door for *any* strangers. Conflicted, my little sister just huddled beside my mother in terror. The paramedics had to break the door down. Fortunately, they reached her in time. She underwent a battery of tests that confirmed benign cysts on her brain. Unable to determine a cause, the doctor concluded the lesions may have been formed from forceps used on her head during childbirth. He said she would have to take the seizure medicine the rest of her life.

Relieved that Mom was now okay, I went back to tending to Maurice, whose drinking was getting worse. It was now March of 2000, and Maurice had just gone on such a severe drinking binge that he had missed several days of work. The situation started taking an even bigger toll on me. I could barely carry on a normal conversation at work, much less write anything. After some coaxing, Maurice's sister Trina got him to check into the State hospital to detox. Keeping him there was no easy feat. She had to halt Maurice from leaving the hospital several times.

"Tell him I love him," I told her.

With someone else now taking care of him, I decided to reach out to my friends. April reassured me that things would get better, but Clarise hit me with a hard dose of reality.

"Sylvia, it's courageous for him to go into detox, but you need to take care of yourself. These problems did not get there overnight, so he's not going to fix them overnight either." In my heart, I knew she was right. With Maurice in the hospital, I was alone with my thoughts. I began to think about the sexual abuse obsessively, and how my anger and sadness had little to do with Maurice and more to do with me not dealing with the molestation from my past.

Maurice got out of the hospital after about a week and was noticeably different. He said they had diagnosed him as manic depressive (today called bipolar). I thought back to his extreme mood changes, and it all started to make sense: Maurice had been self-medicating his mental illness with alcohol. After detox, he seemed more distant and reluctant to spend time with me. It was not a form of contempt for me, but more like he was scared. There was trepidation in his eyes. Sex wasn't the same, either. No one tells you about the debilitating effects that psychotropic drugs have on your sexual organs. As far as I was concerned, sex was the least of our worries, so instead of confronting him about it, I used the time to concentrate on me.

I finally signed up for therapy, and they diagnosed me as clinically depressed. Up until this point, watching "Oprah" was my only therapy, so seeing a psychologist was a major step for me. The therapist wanted to put me on an antidepressant, but I refused, opting for counseling instead. I did, however, tell the therapist I would be open to taking a holistic treatment like St. John's Wort. She didn't know anything about the herb, so we stuck to the counseling.

By April, Maurice was drinking again. In fact, one evening he asked me to go have a drink with him. He tried to validate his reasons for going back to drinking by saying, "I don't like being told what I can and cannot do. I don't believe in absolute anything. Besides, it's just one drink."

Trying to talk him out of it, I gave my "save Maurice" speech: "Think about it this way: The only thing you have is your health. Your career, money, home, car — none of it matters without your health. If you don't have your health, you can't enjoy any of those things."

As usual, my advice fell on closed ears. Maurice's one drink that night led to many more.

Chapter 26

I didn't feel like I was getting much from therapy, but I had been reading a book I discovered in the bookstore, "The Courage to Heal: A Guide for Women Survivors of Child Sexual Abuse." Initially I was intimidated by the book because of its thick width, but once I started reading it, things really started to make sense.

From reading bits and pieces, it seemed I was in what the authors, Ellen Bass and Laura Davis, called the "emergency phase." That meant all I could do was think about the abuse 24/7. I couldn't wait to share what I had read with the therapist. I wanted to share it with Maurice too, but I knew he was too consumed by his own problems to deal with mine.

He was however, concerned about the sharp pains I had been having in my pelvis and took me to the doctor. It turned out I had cysts developing on my ovaries from a hormone imbalance. Apparently my body was producing too much testosterone, causing me to have adult acne, weight fluctuation, excessive body hair and sporadic periods. The doctor told me the cysts could even cause fertility problems. Not one for conventional medicine, I reluctantly started taking the birth control pills she said would regulate my periods and hormones. As distraught as I was over this diagnosis, I realized it was a camouflaged blessing. This condition probably prevented me from conceiving during the many times Maurice and I had unprotected sex, but I didn't dare say that to Maurice. I knew he would take that remark way out of context.

By this time, I started to outgrow the newspaper and began looking for a new job. At the end of May, I finally got a call. Merion Publications, a medical publishing company in King of Prussia, Pennsylvania, was interested in interviewing me for an editorial assistant position. Maurice dropped me off for the job interview and agreed to pick me up when I was finished. Between the testing and the interviews, I was there for three hours! I phoned Maurice to pick me up, only to discover he had never left. He waited in the parking lot in the scorching heat for the entire three hours! When I got in the car, he was drenched in sweat, and I could tell he was a little angry.

After planting a few kisses and hugs on him, he finally cracked a smile. A couple of weeks later, Merion Publications called me for a second interview with the editorial director. I couldn't believe how long the interview process was. After that meeting, days went by. I grew impatient waiting, but Maurice remained optimistic.

"I hope you know you got that job," he said to me one day. Maurice's words couldn't have been more reassuring or accurate. A few days after that conversation, Merion called and offered me the position. To top things off, my supplement at the newspaper had just won first place at the National Newspaper Publisher Association awards, and I received a $250 prize. Talk about going out on top!

Things seemed to be going great all around, even between me and Maurice. In fact, we took another trip to Atlantic City and had a great time, just chilling on the beach and the boardwalk. During this period, I finally felt strong enough to tell him about the sexual abuse I'd experienced. He was the first person in my adulthood I ever told.

"Man, that's FUCKED up," he crooned, shaking his head in disbelief. The intense look in his eyes made me realize he was not prepared for my confession. Maybe telling him had been the wrong thing to do. Just as that thought came to me, he abruptly exited into the living room, smoking the last of his cigarettes. The silence in the next few minutes was loudly deafening. I just knew I had lost him for good. If there was a feeling worse than shame, I felt it right then. I climbed into my bed, and buried my head in the pillows trying to stifle the tears that were now flowing freely down onto my neck. I turned my back to the bedroom's entrance, hunched in a fetal position, and waited for Maurice to walk back in and dump me. Hearing his footsteps, I inhaled deeply and braced myself for the worse.

"Don't cry, baby," he said, climbing into the bed next to me. He slipped his arms around my waist, cradling me from behind. "I am sooo sorry. It's okay. You're going to be okay." He leaned over and kissed my cheek. "I love you, girl."

I let out a sigh of relief! Though he was deeply saddened by my confession, he pledged his support. Sharing my dark secret with him now made me want to open up more in therapy. I switched to a new therapist. No offense to Karen, but I needed someone with a little more edge, someone who would give me more feedback. I was fortunate to get that from my new therapist, Stefanie Brown, a black woman who maintained a diverse patient load. With her encouragement, I also began going to a support group for incest survivors, which was run by a wonderful black woman named Lydia. As a young, black woman, it was imperative for me to know there were other black women out there working with sexual abuse survivors. Somehow, having the two of them in my corner felt very reassuring, and it became less embarrassing for me to be a sexual abuse survivor.

Work was going well, too. I was learning a lot from my new editor, Gertrude. Not only was she a wonderful mentor, she was a genuinely kind person, very easy to talk to both personally and professionally. Everything seemed to be going really well until Maurice dropped another major bombshell: He had accepted a job offer out of state. At first, I thought he was referring to New Jersey, because I knew he had been looking into a job opportunity there. Boy, was I wrong! Maurice had decided to take a position at the "Indianapolis Star." It was the end of 2000, and he was set to start in January of 2001.

I was beyond devastated. I wondered what would happen to us, and I told him so. He mentioned something about my coming with him, but I told him I had just started my own job and wasn't sure I wanted to make such a major move so soon. For the next few weeks, up until his departure, I cried whenever I saw him, which made him tear up too.

"Do you want me to stay?" he finally asked.

"Yes," I responded, "but I know you wouldn't be happy if you turned down this job."

"You're right," he admitted.

While Maurice finalized his moving plans, I worked with the newspaper's secretary to plan his going away party. Initially, Maurice was not feeling this idea, but when all was planned and executed, he was quite touched by the gesture. Maurice was tough as nails on the surface, but inside he was truly a softy. When we got home, Maurice couldn't stop talking about his party. He was like an animated kid. I was so happy to see him that giddy. Maurice made his transition to Indianapolis in January and, somehow, I couldn't help but feel it was a terrible mistake. However, I pushed those thoughts out of my mind and decided to concentrate on my own recovery.

Chapter 27

Although I began attending the support group, I still hadn't formed the connection I had hoped for. I felt at a loss. Why the heck was I there? On the surface I knew alcoholics were recovering from alcohol addiction and smokers from nicotine in their 12-step groups, but I still didn't understand what incest survivors were recovering from. There wasn't an identifiable substance to remove from our lives — I mean, you can't take the abuse back.

I finally gained some clarity during the third meeting. As if reading my mind, Lydia, the group's leader, remarked, "Incest survivors are recovering from being victims." Once she said that, it was as if someone handed me the key to a locked treasure chest. It all finally made sense. That's why I was there, to recover from being a victim; to erase the victim mentality.

From the point I was initially molested at the age of five, I had begun behaving as a victim. I took on that persona in every friendship, relationship and interaction I had with others. Through the group, therapy and the book, I began to understand that I had misplaced anger. Instead of directing the anger at my perpetrators, I had made everyone else around me pay for what they had done. If you were in my life, you had to walk on egg shells, because if you did something or said something I didn't like, I'd cut you off. It was easier to cut someone off than show emotion or risk exposing the intimate side of myself.

Around this time, everything I saw on TV seemed to center around sexual abuse, as if it was waiting for me to tune in. One evening I watched a therapist counseling a sexual abuse survivor: "Your emotional development stops at the age you were molested. You don't develop empathy." Although he was counseling another survivor, I felt as if he were talking directly to me. For so long, I had wondered why I resorted to juvenile behavior with friends and family. My abuse had started at five. Hearing the therapist, I realized I had been dealing with my problems with a five-year-old's mentality. Though intellectually very intelligent, I was emotionally bankrupt and had not developed the emotional maturity of an adult to process what had happened to me. For the first time in my life, I was starting to understand that the abuse was not my fault. Listening to the other survivors share in the support group, I suddenly recognized the true extent of the emotional damage.

As more memories started to come back, I began to understand not only why I was so unhappy, but why I thought the way I did. For instance, during the time my cousin Pony was molesting me, I remember the Clarence Thomas/Anita Hill sexual harassment trial was going on. My family and I watched every minute of that trial like it was a TV show. Personally, I didn't know what to make of the allegations, but I vividly remember my grandmother's opinion.

"She's a lie!" she shouted to no one in particular in her broken Southern grammar. I'm sure my grandmother didn't think much about that remark after she said it, but it sure stuck with me. I thought to myself, if she could not believe a stranger like Anita Hill, why would she believe me, her own granddaughter? Would the rest of the family think like she did?

Remembering this story made me think of a passage from "The Courage to Heal" book: "When a group of people has [historically] been oppressed and discriminated against, there is a need to maintain a united front. This can make it more difficult to acknowledge abuse within the group." Perhaps this is why my grandmother sided with Clarence Thomas. Maybe she did not want to see black people airing their dirty laundry on national television.

Up to now in my life, I could sit with a roomful of friends and still feel lonely. I didn't know it at the time, but what I was feeling was depression. I'd often leave early or skip the outings altogether so I wouldn't have to deal with such debilitating emotions. My friends and family thought I was being aloof. "She just has an attitude," they would say, but they didn't understand how much pain I was really in or how paralyzed I felt in my own life. I couldn't understand it either. Who knew the sadness I was feeling stemmed from the abuse I had subconsciously suppressed from my memory.

Listening to the survivors' share in the group, I began to see that others did have the same feelings. Knowing that people from various

"Creating a New Normal: Cleaning Up a Dysfunctional Life"

backgrounds experienced sexual abuse, made me feel less abnormal. It gave me promise and hope for recovery. I have to admit I didn't get the point of 12-step groups until I found the one for incest survivors. Ironically, I thought back to my conversation with the counselor on the alcohol abuse hotline. "No one can recover on their own," she had said. I finally understood the universal meaning of those words. Black, White, Latino, Asian — we are all here to help each other.

****

Around this same time, I experienced an epiphany that changed my life and the way I viewed recovery. A few months earlier, my friend Manny had given me a journal with the "Footprints" poem on its cover. Although I had seen this spiritual prose many times, I had never bothered to read it. As I took the journal out to pen my first entry, I glanced at the footprints on the cover and read the poem. By the time I got to the last line, I realized its true meaning: God had never abandoned me after the sexual abuse, as I had so subconsciously thought. Rather, He had been carrying me all along.

When I thought about the death of my sister and being homeless and cheated on, I realized I didn't get myself through those heartaches by myself. God did. He carried me when I could not carry myself, just like the man in "Footprints." He carried me when I did not want to go on, when I wanted to end my relationship with my mother, when I did not want to let Maurice move out of state, when I did not know where my next meal or place to sleep would come from. He was what I had referred to as my conscience all those years. And, most importantly, He didn't leave me when we left organized religion. For so long, I had felt intensely unworthy of His love because I did not belong to any formal religion. I felt even more validated about this epiphany when I learned that one of the 12 steps in the support group encouraged belief in a higher power.

****

Around this same time, I enrolled in a hypnotherapy class. This was very strange for me because I had absolutely no belief or even an interest in stuff like hypnosis. As far as I was concerned, these "shams" were for the weirdos on TV. Yet for some reason, I was drawn to that class, so against all logic, I enrolled. At this point, my recovery had taught me that I had to keep stepping out of my comfort zone to heal fully.

It didn't take long to find out that I had grossly misunderstood the intent of this class. Amazingly, it was there that I learned how to control my thoughts. Up until this point, I always behaved and thought like a victim. When things happened to me that I didn't like, or if someone said something to me I disagreed with, I'd take it personally and let it affect my feelings about myself for the rest of the day.

We studied a book called "The Power of Your Subconscious Mind," by Dr. Joseph Murphy. Throughout the book, I learned the difference between the conscious and subconscious mind. I learned that the conscious mind is where we do all of our active thinking, and where we form opinions, logic and reason. It, in fact, controls what enters our subconscious mind. Unlike the conscious mind, the subconscious is passive. It puts those ideas/thoughts from the conscious mind into action by ensuring that every thought is carried out or manifested in our physical world. In other words, the subconscious does not know the difference between right and wrong and, therefore, will do exactly what we tell it to do through our *most repetitious* thoughts.

For instance, suppose you turn on your favorite radio station, and there's a new song playing. You don't know the words, but after hearing the song several times, you find yourself singing along. When did you learn the words? You didn't get a sheet of music with the lyrics, so there's only one plausible way you could have memorized the lyrics — using your subconscious mind. Your subconscious mind didn't ask you whether or not you liked the song, it just memorized it through the repetition of continuous radio playing. That's the way your subconscious mind works, through repetition. If it sees or hears a message long enough, it will accept it as being true.

The same example applies to the parent/child relationship — especially when a child wants something he or she can't have. The child is more likely to get a "yes" from a parent when the adult is in a tired, relaxed or sleepy state, rather than when the parent is alert. If this were true, I thought to myself, then how could I take control of my thinking. The instructor, Joan Bracey, taught us how to control those thoughts by making positive affirmations right before sleep. This, she said, was important because the subconscious is more controllable when it is in a passive state, like sleep. Still, I was skeptical. As far as I was concerned, that affirmation stuff didn't work. I had been reading self-help books for years, and their hokey affirmations never worked for me. However, I had never tried the process in such a specific manner as Joan suggested.

Eventually, I stopped fighting with myself, which wasn't easy. I had to really open myself up to try something like this, to step out of my small emotional box. I finally reasoned I had nothing to lose. Like "The Courage to Heal" authors said, the worst (the abuse itself) was already over. In my heart, I knew the only thing that stood in the way of full recovery was my own destructive thinking.

Joan, perhaps sensing our skepticism, gave us a simple exercise to do before having us use the affirmations. She told us to give ourselves a wake-up time for the following morning. We were instructed to verbally repeat this wake up time several times before bed. I really wanted to test her theory, so I gave myself an unusual wake-up time. Normally, I rise at 5 a.m., so I set my "internal" clock for 4 a.m.

Remarkably, I woke up at exactly 4 a.m. the next morning! Perhaps, there was something to this "unusual" method after all!

I began using affirmations prior to sleep for everything that I needed. I even recorded specific affirmations on a tape recorder that I listened to each night as I slept. One by one, I received help in every area I requested, from help paying bills to controlling my anger. What I was learning was what Rhonda Byrne's would describe years later in her book/DVD as "The Secret," or the law of attraction.

As I continued with Joan's class, I also learned another valuable lesson. How you label yourself is extremely important. I had always considered myself a victim, but as my time with the group and class grew, I began to see myself as a survivor. Each time we introduced ourselves to the group (which was required at each meeting), I'd say, "Hi, My name is Sylvia, and I'm an incest survivor." I'm sure that ongoing repetition seeped into my subconscious, because my behavior began to drastically change for the better.

The biggest modification I noticed was that I became less fearful. I reconnected with old friends and easily made new ones. I started going out more and sharing my feelings. I even started to smile more. Every area of my life improved significantly, except my love life.

Chapter 28

During the spring of 2001, I made my first visit to Indianapolis, Indiana, to visit Maurice. Although he was friendly with a few co-workers, he still had not made any friends, so he was very happy to see me, and I was ecstatic to see him.

Every day was chock full of fun during the two weeks I spent there, going everywhere from the zoo, out to dinner, to a show and to the movies. I even went to work with Maurice a couple of times. He was doing pretty well. In the few months he had been there, he found a counselor and an AA support group. He had even stopped smoking weed. Everything seemed so promising. I didn't want our visit to end. Before I left, I brought Maurice one of those fish bowls that comes with the plant on top and a Fat Albert navy blue t-shirt. You would have thought it was Christmas the way his eyes lit up when he saw those gifts. On our way to the airport, we stopped by a local waterfall fountain and took some pictures together. I didn't want to leave and was trying hard to suck up my tears.

By the time we arrived at the airport, I was a mess. Tears were streaming down my face and onto my shirt. Maurice didn't like seeing me cry because it made him sad. Each time he tried to console me, my tears would flow even harder. Maurice teared up too.

"I love you, girl," he said and pressed his lips against my forehead. It was time for me to go. "Goodbye," I whispered.

"Not goodbye," he replied. "See ya later."

Over the next few months, we both tried to keep ourselves preoccupied with work. My positive thinking was really paying off at my job. Somehow I got the guts to propose becoming a columnist. I suggested a monthly editorial for minorities. Management thought it was a brilliant idea! To top things off, I received first place for a story I had written on Washington, DC homeless. Not long after that they promoted me to assistant editor. I also started travel for the company to cover different industry conferences. The travel time gave me the extra days I needed to take off and visit Maurice more regularly. Each time we saw each other, it was hard to part, especially when my visits were short.

"Why don't you move out there?" his mother asked me one day. Good question, I thought. Maurice and I were missing each other immensely, and I had been flying back and forth from Indianapolis for months now. I guess I still had reservations because there were two things bothering me about relocating to be with Maurice. First of all, I didn't see the point in moving in with someone without being married or at least engaged. Secondly, Maurice had started drinking again. With no family and friends around to support him, his drinking had tripled while he continued taking the anxiety pills.

He tried to conceal the change from me, but I could tell. Besides, I could smell the booze through his skin, and our sex life became nonexistent because of the pills and the booze. This really affected Maurice's self-esteem — he felt like he was less of a man because we couldn't be intimate. One evening, I had to rush with him to the hospital because his liver was hurting so bad from drinking. Besides work, my visits and occasional outings with co-workers, Maurice remained isolated. He had even stopped going to AA. Eventually he became more distant toward me, too. On my last visit, Maurice asked me to move in with him. I told him we needed to create a healthier relationship for me to make that decision. When I got back to Philadelphia, I called him and suggested we come up with a plan to help him quit drinking. Maurice refused to talk about it, and I told him I couldn't keep visiting him while he was still living that lifestyle.

He was upset about my decision because I had never been that stern with him before. With my renewed attitude, God had given me the courage to speak the tough words that were long overdue. Over the next year, 2002, we continued our relationship over the phone. I pleaded with Maurice to come back to Pennsylvania. He admitted he was not happy in Indiana, but did not want to leave and look like a failure.

Conflicted with emotions, I did not want to stop the lines of communication. Maurice was never really a phone person, so we didn't talk often. When we did, Maurice was usually intoxicated. One day, he called me unexpectedly and said, "Do you still have my picture up?" I almost dropped the phone. A few days earlier, I had taken his picture down in frustration about our problems. How could he have possibly known? I didn't want to hurt his feelings, but I also didn't want to lie to him.

"No," I said weakly. "I took it down."

"I thought so."

"Why did you ask?"

"I just had a feeling."

I shouldn't have been surprised by his question. This was just another example of the unusual bond Maurice and I had. We could sense things about each other, even when we were apart. Although our relationship wasn't what it used to be, Maurice and I still really loved each other. However, my life had changed significantly while he was away. I was now running my own support group for incest survivors. No longer feeling like a victim, I did not want to be Maurice's enabler. I prayed to God asking Him to give me an amicable way to remove myself from Maurice's life, so he could heal.

Soon after that prayer, Maurice called and said it was okay for me to leave him if I ever felt he was becoming a burden. I declined the offer. It wasn't until I got off the phone that I realized this had been the amicable opportunity I had so diligently prayed for — but now had just let slip away. In 2003, Maurice and I agreed to put more effort into our relationship. Despite imploring from me, his sister and mother, it was Maurice's father who convinced him it was time to come back to Pennsylvania. I was really ecstatic about that! Things seemed to be looking up again. We had even resumed talk about marriage.

Meanwhile, I ended the support group to volunteer with a local community education program to teach a workshop for black sexual abuse survivors. Teaching felt empowering and therapeutic! It enabled me to give back what others like Lydia from the support group and my therapist, Dr. Brown, had given me. I knew it was important to share what I learned with other black sexual abuse survivors even though it was still a taboo subject in our community. However, it appeared it would take a while for others to share my passion, because only one student signed up for the class. Nonetheless, I was not dismayed. I taught that one student with as much passion as I would have had for 20.

During this time, Maurice and I were busy trying to readjust to our relationship. We had not seen each other in a year. Maurice had lost a lot of weight and was concerned about what I would think of his new physique. Despite the weight loss, Maurice was still the sexy man I had first met four years ago. It was hard to believe we had been together for that long! Our first date after his return went very well. For a while we smothered each other kissing, embracing and staring at each other because we were both so overwhelmed with emotion.

Maurice always liked quiet places, so we ate at a local diner, then spent the rest of the evening talking in my apartment. He always liked when I massaged his scalp, so he laid his head in my lap for a rubdown. Somehow it made him feel both relaxed and secure. I could sense him starting to get comfortable, but I could also tell something was bothering him.

"You know," he said. "I don't see a light at the end of the tunnel for me."

I winced at him, but tried to hide my shock and give him some words of encouragement.

"Don't worry; it's there," I said, trying to reassure both him and me that he would be okay.

Over the next several weeks, things seemed to be going fine. We were getting back into a regular routine with each other. When Maurice had left Indianapolis, he did not have another job lined up, so he began searching for employment. It was April 2003, a little over a month since he had been back.

Maurice and I went out on another date, but there was an awkward silence between us. I think we both had a lot on our minds. I was elated to have Maurice home, but I had changed a great deal during the time he was away. I knew I couldn't deal with the alcoholism this time around, and I wondered if he was still drinking as heavily as he had been before, so I was a bit apprehensive on our date and it showed.

As if reading my mind, he said, "You know, this is the first date I've been on with you where I haven't been drunk."

I didn't know whether to be relieved or angry. Did his confession mean he was never himself throughout our four-and-a-half-year relationship? Was he always intoxicated? It really weighed heavily on my mind, and I couldn't get into the rest of our date. Plus, Maurice had also cussed out a guy while we were waiting in line for our food, so my already lukewarm mood quickly became even less enthusiastic. Maurice sensed the change and reluctantly took me home early.

After that date, I questioned our relationship once again, but didn't feel I could go to Maurice with my concerns. He knew there was something wrong and called me up that same weekend to straighten things out. I could tell he was drunk when he called, but I agreed to let him come over. When he got to my apartment, he smelled like a cross between a winery and a sewer. I had seen Maurice drunk plenty of times, but not like this. Maurice was more of a functional alcoholic, so he was fairly good at hiding his drinking. This time was very different. He was so incoherent that I was surprised he had even been able to drive over to my apartment.

I decided it was best for him to sleep some of the alcohol off before we talked, but he kept trying to discuss our previous date. A lot of what he was saying was very cryptic, barely comprehensible in his drunken state. Then he started talking to himself, which really freaked me out because I had never seen him do that. Eventually he drifted off to sleep, but the sleep did little to make him sober. I tried talking about his drinking and its effect on our relationship, but he kept changing the subject. Somehow, Maurice was convinced I was seeing someone else.

"That's not true," I assured him. Anyone who knew me knew that I was fiercely devoted to him, even when he was miles away. I really wanted things to work out with him and, though very frustrated, I had not given up hope. We ended up arguing. Our conversation was going around in circles, so Maurice left. "You don't have to ever worry about seeing me again," he yelled as he sprinted down my steps.

I followed him out the door. "I knew you were going to do this!" I screamed back. "I knew you were going to walk away from me." I turned to go back up the stairs as he stormed off to his car. I could still hear him yelling as I climbed back up the stairs. "Imani? Imani? Wait!" he said, shouting my nickname.

I swirled on my heels to come back, when I heard, "Fuck you!"

Hearing that, I went back into my apartment before he had a chance to see me. He was not going to embarrass me out in the street. As far as I was concerned, we were through. I had made up my mind, I would not be around him again until he got his act together. Over the next several days, I did not hear from Maurice. I thought it was only a matter of time before he called to apologize, but those weeks turned into months, and still there was no word from him. I tried not to get too concerned, since we had been down this road before — breaking up for weeks or months at a time, not talking and then getting back together. I figured Maurice was taking this time to focus on his recovery and, recalling my conversation with the addictions counselor, I felt it best to keep my distance and let his family take care of him. I knew they loved him and would never let anything bad happen to him. Besides, if he were in serious trouble, I knew they would call.

Although I considered it plenty of times, I decided against calling. For his sake (and my sanity), I knew I could no longer enable him. However, I still held out hope that I would run into him on the street. Plus, I knew several of my former co-workers had been in touch with him, so I figured it was only a matter of time before he called me. Despite all of this consternation, I still loved Maurice. I don't know how I knew, but I knew he still loved me, too. Like I said, Maurice and I had a strong connection that often transcended words.

I believe he still felt a lot of shame, guilt and hopelessness, because he called our old newspaper asking for his job back. When word got back to me about it, I knew he was feeling desperate, because he had vowed to never go back to that company. Unfortunately, they didn't rehire him. Apparently, they thought it would be too risky to bring him back. I knew Maurice didn't like rejection, so I'm sure he didn't handle the blow well.

****

I was concerned about Maurice, but I was doing extremely well in other areas of my life. I reconnected with my old high school boyfriend, Barry, from surfing on Classmates.com. We were both excited to be talking again. So much had changed. Barry, who had gone through a spiritual transformation, was going by the name, Ishmael. He also had a toddler, a girl named Naomi. Though we did not get back together, Ishmael and I formed a really great friendship on the phone over the next few months.

Work was also going well. I had received another writing award at work, and had just wrapped up my second workshop, which had expanded to four more people! Though it was not a full room, I took the increase as a sign of good things to come, because the participants loved the workshop. I felt more empowered than ever and knew I was progressing well. I was actually making and keeping goals. Just weeks before my 28th birthday, I finally got my driver's license. I felt really liberated! When my birthday rolled around, I thought I was going to hear from Maurice for sure, but it didn't happen. As always, I continued to keep Maurice in my prayers. In fact, I found myself praying for him a lot more than usual.

****

Then came November 21, 2003; it was a Friday night, and I was up watching the Soul Train Awards. Alicia Keys was debuting her new song, "You Don't Know My Name." Normally I was enthusiastic about the awards, but that night, I was feeling really down, almost depressed. An unshakable sadness settled inside me. It was the type of sadness punctuated with fear that anchors in the pit of your belly. Something was definitely wrong. I tried to push the feeling away, but it persisted. I literally felt like I was on the verge of tears, as if I had been emotionally wounded. What was wrong with me? Why would I feel this miserable for no reason? I decided to pray. Just when I thought the feeling was passing, I experienced a weird sensation like someone had ripped out the bottom of my stomach and robbed me of my joy. Feeling overwhelmed, I went to bed early, hoping I would feel better in the morning.

When I woke, I did feel a little better. The intense sadness was gone, but I still felt like something was still wrong. I dismissed the thought and went on about my day, running errands. It was around 1 or 2 p.m. when I decided to check my voicemail. There was a message from Trina, Maurice's sister. She said to give her a call when I got in. I was happy to hear the sound of her voice. I had missed being around her. I immediately called Trina back. A stranger answered. It was Maurice's Aunt Ellen. She explained it wasn't a good time to call.

I could hear Maurice's mother in the background asking, "Who is it?"

"Sylvia," Aunt Ellen responded.

"I need to take this call," Maurice's mom said in the background.

"Sylvia?" she said when she picked up the phone.

"Hi, Mrs. Richards!" I beamed. "How are you?"

"Not good," she whispered.

"What's wrong?"

"Sylvia, baby…He's gone."

"Gone?" I repeated. "Who?"

"Maurice."

"What do you mean gone? Gone away? Where did he go?" I kept repeating the words, as that sinking feeling returned to my stomach.

"Here, I'll let you speak to Trina."

"Sylvia, Maurice passed away," Trina said. "We found him this morning."

"WHAT!!!" I shrieked. "WHAT DO YOU MEAN?!!!"

Trina said their mother had found him that morning, cold and still. Apparently he died in his sleep. She shook him, but he didn't respond. Apparently, everyone had been in denial, because Maurice's father suggested all he needed was a shot to wake him up. They finally called the EMT, who came and confirmed his death.

Immediately all of my emotions from the previous night returned. Tears and snot simultaneously raced down my face. I could not comprehend what I was hearing! It just couldn't be true. Maurice was *supposed* to get better. I had been praying for God to save him, to take me out of his life, so he could recover and heal. It had to be a mistake.

I tried desperately to wrap my brain around what was happening, but I could barely think, let alone hold myself upright. I felt as if someone had hurled bricks at my gut. I just did not want to believe the man I loved was gone, less than a week before his first 31st birthday. He was the last person I had ever expected to lose.

Chapter 29

I know now that I would never have gotten through those first few months after Maurice's death had it not been for his family. In fact, it was his mother, sick with her own grief, who gave me comfort in the initial days following his death.

"You know, Maurice really loved you," she said the day after he passed away. Although I was sure Maurice never stopped loving me, it felt reassuring to hear it directly from her. I loved Maurice's mom as if she were my own mother, and I'm certain she loved me like a daughter. And here she was comforting me, when I should have been comforting her. In the four years that I had known her, she had lost her mother, her sister and, now, her only son. I could not comprehend what kept her so sane.

Despite their tragedy, she and her family sensed my heartache and took me into their home. For the first few months, I spent most of my weekends there, where they fed me and kept me preoccupied. In fact, they were among the few people I could talk to about my pain. Unfortunately, there wasn't a grief support group around for young people like myself; and my friends and co-workers, hard as they tried, couldn't relate to what I was going through. They could not understand how I could grieve over a man who a) I had not seen in months and b) was an alcoholic. They just wanted the "old Sylvia" back as quickly as possible. I tried to explain to them that was not likely. The "normal" I had known was gone forever. No longer could I cling to the hope that Maurice and I would reconcile. I had to create a "new normal," a new way of living because my heart was still very much attached to Maurice. During this time, I told those friends who didn't understand that I would be taking some time away from my usual activities, and that they shouldn't take my absence personally. Some got it; others didn't and were very offended.

Many thought I was in complete isolation. On the contrary; if there was one thing my recovery from incest had taught me, it was that I needed a support system. I know for a fact I would not have reached out to anyone had I not had that prior healing experience with therapy and a 12-step group. I would have coped in isolation, like I had done for so many years after the sexual abuse. As devastated as I was, God gave me the strength to surround myself with those who understood and could help me deal with the grief. Those people included my therapist, Maurice's family, my dear friend Tamal, my mother surprisingly, and my old friend, Melody.

Dr. Brown said that teaching a class for sexual abuse survivors would be challenging during this time, so I suspended my workshop. Having worked with me for so long, she knew that the added stress would aggravate my recovery. Going through the grief felt like a re-victimization — not in a sexual way but as if I had been robbed of more time with Maurice, of the possibility of a healthy Maurice. Death felt like a perpetrator, robbing me of joy and leaving me once again to suffer in its aftermath. Most of all, I felt guilt and anger for not having an opportunity to tell Maurice how much I loved him. Maurice relied heavily on external validation, and I couldn't help but think how he had probably convinced himself he was unworthy of my love and love in general. I especially felt this way in those first few months of grief. I still had so many unanswered questions.

****

How I felt spiritually was by far the worst emotion for me to sort through. Although I still believed in God, I struggled with what to believe about life after death, especially in the wake of Maurice's passing. I needed to know if I would see Maurice again in the afterlife. As far as I was concerned, I could not come to terms with his death until I found the answer. Even though I was no longer a Jehovah's Witness, I still believed as they did about life after death.

As I mentioned earlier, Jehovah's Witnesses believe that only 144,000 pre-selected servants of God go to heaven when they die. The remaining righteous (faithful Jehovah's Witnesses) are resurrected to a paradise on earth after God destroys the wicked people from the world. Intellectually, I knew of other spiritual beliefs about life after death, but the beliefs of Jehovah's Witnesses' were so ingrained in me from my childhood that it was hard to emotionally and spiritually believe in anything else. Since I was no longer a Jehovah's Witness and I did not believe that others besides the 144,000 went to heaven, where did that leave me? Where did that leave Maurice, who was Catholic? Would I see him again? Was there life after death for people with no official religious denomination like me?

It was hard to share these thoughts with friends, even the ones who were very supportive. None of them understood the Jehovah's Witness faith or how challenging it was to believe anything other than what I had been taught since birth. It's funny, you don't recognize how extremely important your spiritual beliefs are in your ability to heal until you lose someone very close to you. Some of my friends tried to convince me that all, including Maurice, went to heaven. While others wondered what the big deal was. Why, they asked, did it even matter what happened after you died?

They could not understand how unfinished I felt our relationship was, that I still had more to say to Maurice, or how tortured my soul felt without him. No one could explain the deep, continuous anguish you feel when you lose someone that close. Even on joyous occasions, you always feel like something, rather someone, is missing. No one understood how I could love someone who drank himself to death or that I could love someone who had been so emotionally conflicted. During this time, I noticed how easy it was for people I knew to be judgmental, how simple it was to hypothesize about what I should and should not believe. Initially, I was offended by this reaction and pushed them away, but later, months later, I realized these people were not trying to offend me or hurt me. Rather, they just did not know what to say or do to help me. Many, who were young like me, could relate to the death of a grandparent or a distant relative, but not to the loss of a partner.

True, Maurice was a tortured soul with a lot of self-inflicted pain. But even the most tortured soul is loved by somebody. Sometimes we humans forget how imperfect we *all* are. It becomes easy to judge those we do not like or do not know, as was the case of my friends judging Maurice. The fact is that despite his flaws, Maurice was unconditionally loved by a mother, father, grandfather, two sisters, aunts, uncles, cousins, a best friend and me. We knew he was a loving man, who at times made irrational choices when scared. So many of us hide behind fear and then express it in negative ways: overeating, using drugs, working long hours, being promiscuous, and yes, drinking heavily.

Right or wrong, I reminded my friends, this was the man I chose to love, and yes, I had to deal with the consequences of that choice. I could not erase the past even if I wanted to. And right or wrong, I desperately wanted them to acknowledge my emotions. I didn't need them to debate the authenticity of my love for Maurice, but I wanted them to respect my right to grieve. As the months went by, however, I began to realize that I could not seek external validation from my loved ones; rather, I had to create a "new normal" to heal myself.

Chapter 30

I cried every day for the first six months after his death. However, the sorrow began to lessen as the first year continued. Although my love for Maurice remained the same, I started to come to terms with his passing.

During our relationship, I had discussed with him how much I wanted to go to massage school, so I could open a holistic day spa. I also wanted to go to massage school so I could learn a technique I had read about called Amanae,® a type of bodywork that helps people with trauma like sexual abuse release the old emotional wounds. In the weeks that preceded his death, I had already taken steps to enroll. Since I knew massage made up the bulk of the spa business, my goal was to become a licensed massage therapist and build a clientele, then add other spa services and staff. When Maurice passed, I was so consumed with grief that I almost abandoned this dream, but then, just like the poem "Footprints," God pushed me forward, and I enrolled.

The nine-month program was a pleasant distraction during the grieving process, because it gave me an opportunity to focus on something else besides the agony of losing Maurice. I especially liked the fact that the school was very holistic and included a lot of alternative modalities. The school's inclusion of meditation, grounding and self-care techniques became instrumental in my recovery. Slowly, I began to regain my confidence and strength.

Creating a new normal meant I could no longer attach myself to things that did not fulfill me, and that included my job. In the months succeeding Maurice's death, I had become increasingly detached from my job. Although I loved writing, I no longer desired to do it in such a structured, corporate environment. I was frustrated trying to write articles that advertisers then edited to their liking. Emotionally, it also was hard to be around my young, married co-workers when they discussed their families. In fact, those events were impossible to escape. The large company I worked for was notorious for celebrating every engagement and birth announcement.

Being around those conversations and events were constant reminders of what I had lost. I tried to explain this feeling to my boss when she confronted me about my declining job performance, but she could not understand. In July 2004, on my four-year anniversary, I resigned and took a position at a physical therapy practice in the city. Unable to secure steady employment for me, the company let me go after only three months of work. They told me to re-apply next year, if a position became available.

****

Fortunately, my massage school posted regular employment openings. One of those postings offered a massage room to rent two days a week for $100 a month. I immediately jumped on the opportunity! However, it was challenging trying to build my own clientele. I was only able to maintain 10-15 clients per month. To make a living in the massage business, you need to do 10-15 clients a week. Backed into a corner, I reluctantly signed up for unemployment. While on unemployment, I became very complacent. With now a steady check coming in, I didn't work as hard to maintain my massage clientele. It was easy to retreat once again into "victim" mode. I blamed my inability to retain clients on the clients themselves, calling the massage field unpredictable.

A year had now passed since Maurice died. Although I wasn't crying every day, I developed other unhealthy coping mechanisms. I didn't recognize my destructive behavior then, but I was eating uncontrollably and watching hours and hours of senseless television. I became especially hooked on soap operas and rental movies. It didn't take long for me to pack on the pounds. When Maurice passed, I had weighed 125 lbs. Over the next few months, I added 30 pounds to my 4 feet 11 inch frame. By March 2005, I was 155 lbs. Many of my friends didn't see me during this time. If I wasn't renting a movie or going to get fast food, I rarely left the house. When I did, I camouflaged my weight gain well. Since it was winter, all I had to do was wear black and layer my clothing.

I hate to say it, but I don't think I would have gotten out of that funk if my mother hadn't become ill. Now crippled with arthritis in her knees, she was in constant, debilitating pain. Apparently the cartilage had worn down completely in her knees, to the point where bone was rubbing on bone. The doctor told her she had to get not one, but two knee replacements. The surgeon scheduled the procedure for March 28, 2005. My mother would not be able to return to work for at least two months. My little sister, then only 10, was too young to take care of Mom by herself, so I left Philly and set up temporary residence in Boston with them. My mother's recovery was long and grueling. She had so many complications from the surgery that they had to keep her hospitalized for nearly three weeks. That did not sit well with her. She gave the staff hell from the moment she checked in until the day she left.

Meanwhile, I was busy trying to re-adjust to Boston and my new family responsibilities. I was now my sister's primary caretaker, which was no easy feat. Though she was excited to have her big sister home, she was not prepared to take orders from me, so we clashed frequently in the beginning. Having lived alone for so long, I was overwhelmed with my new tasks. I didn't know raising a child could be so challenging! I was constantly transporting Sarah from one activity to the next or going to a parent/teacher meeting. In addition, I had to pay bills, rent and shop for groceries.

To further complicate matters, I was traveling back and forth to Philadelphia every other weekend to see massage clients and manage my own bills. I was completely exhausted! I thought things would get a little easier when my mother was released from the hospital, but I was wrong. When she wasn't having physical therapy, she was confined to bed, which meant I had to do everything for her and my sister. Despite the strong painkillers Mom was on, she still experienced pain around the clock. I was constantly getting up throughout the night to readjust her position and administer more ice packs or pain meds. During the day, I ran her errands, took her to doctor's appointments or tended to household chores. By the end of the day, I was pooped. No one ever tells you that being a caretaker comes with so many intense responsibilities.

As exhausting as my schedule was, I have to admit that it got me moving and out of my previous funk. I hadn't lived with my family in years, so being a caretaker gave me an opportunity to reconnect with them. And even though we clashed on many occasions, we still enjoyed each other's company. I got the opportunity to take my sister on several outings, and my mother and I enjoyed shooting the breeze with each other like "old girlfriends." In fact, my mother became one of my biggest supporters in my recovery from sexual abuse. Looking at us now, it is nearly unfathomable to believe we were once so estranged. I was also able to reconnect with my "extended relatives," Melody and her family. Melody, the second oldest of six siblings and now a foster mother, was more accustomed to children than I was, so she was a tremendous help with my new responsibilities. If I needed a ride, a baby-sitter or an ear to listen to me, she was there.

I even got the chance to reconnect with some old friends, including my ex-boyfriend Ishmael, whom I had not spoken to in months. Ishmael was still as gracious and confident as I remembered him, so it was very easy to be attracted to this man all over again. Although there was still a definite mutual attraction between us, it still wasn't strong enough to resume a romantic relationship. In the past, this realization would have crushed me, and I probably would have stopped being around him. But now, having been through so much and having a greater understanding of self, I remained cool. I was just grateful to have developed a real interest in someone other than Maurice since his passing. Today, Ishmael and I are still good friends.

I even had the opportunity to connect with my old friend, Andrea, who now has a burgeoning career in entertainment thanks to a stint as the first black woman on "The Biggest Loser."

I even reconnected with my old college buddy, Micha, who now has a legit job and is married with a son. I ended up staying in Boston for four months to help my mother recover. By this time, I had formed a tight bond with both friends and family. I was reluctant to leave, but knew I had to get back to my own life in Philadelphia.

Chapter 31

Transitioning back to life back in Philly was not easy. My unemployment had run out, my clientele had dried up, and I was having a difficult time finding a job. Fortunately, God placed some lifesavers in my corner. My mother, who had gone back to work, helped me pay several bills. My landlord's office gave me some leeway with the rent. My good friend, Tamal, a social worker, hooked me up with some emergency community resources from a food bank, so I wouldn't starve. He even let me use his own laundry facilities since I didn't have any money.

Despite all the obstacles, God helped me endure. Having been homeless before and dealt with so much grief, I knew God would not leave me hanging. Instead of wallowing in my despair, I realized He kept me motivated. The survivor in me kicked in. I was creating a "new normal," learning to trust again and opening myself up to new opportunities around me. During this time, I did a lot of reading. I came across a book in the bookstore called, "Secrets of the Millionaire Mind: Mastering the Inner Game of Wealth," by T. Harv Eker.

Throughout the book, the author noted the most distinguishing characteristics between the way successful people think and the way poor people think. Although there were many notable traits, five had the most profound effect on me: First, he wrote, "People are scared to death of failure, but they're even more frightened of success." This was a true eye opener for me. If I was to experience real healing, I had to stop procrastinating and second guessing every decision.

Second, he said, "For most people, the conditioning of punishment is so ingrained that, even if there's no one around to punish them when they make a mistake, they subconsciously punish themselves." This was the case with how I dealt with the aftermath of the sexual abuse. Even though I had not seen either of my perpetrators in years, I was still punishing myself by isolating myself from friends and overeating.

Third, the author said, "It's not the size of the challenge; it's the size of you." Had I really let these challenges in my life become bigger than my will to have a healthy life? If I did, how would I rebuild myself, emotionally, physically and spiritually? The answer appeared in the author's fourth point: "If you are willing to do only what's easy," he wrote, "life will be hard. But, if you are willing to do what's hard, life will be easy." For me, that directive meant doing the very things I had been most reluctant to do, namely, eat right, exercise and turn off the television. To make progress, I had to get tough with myself. To do this, I began keeping a journal of my daily activities, taking note of not just the acts themselves but jotting down my thoughts in the moment.

"No thought lives in your mind rent-free," the author declared in the fifth point. "Meaning you will pay for negative thoughts. You will pay either in money, energy, time, health or in your level of happiness." Keeping a journal helped me understand not only what my specific distractions were, but how they affected me. One of the things I noticed was how easy it was to talk myself out of initiating and completing a task. I also took note of how bored I got with a routine and how difficult it was for me to try something new.

Armed with these new revelations, I devised a plan. First, I decided that whenever a positive goal entered my thoughts, I had to act on it immediately within the first two minutes. I picked the time period of two minutes because when I tracked my distractions, I noticed it only took two minutes to talk myself out of doing something productive. This realization meant I had to retrain my brain. To do that, I had to re-apply the techniques I had learned from Joan's class three years earlier to what I wanted to accomplish now.

This choice enabled me to jumpstart my daily workouts. I love to walk, so I made a commitment to rise by 6 a.m. and walk an hour down to the pier daily. I alternated this schedule with exercising on my elliptical at home so I wouldn't get bored with the workouts. Changing my diet, however, was much more challenging. Working out made me even hungrier. To help control my hunger, I used protein shakes between meals to satisfy my intense cravings. I traded my usual breakfast of pancakes and turkey sausage for bananas and oatmeal. Lunch was usually a tuna or grilled chicken salad, and dinner was baked chicken with steamed veggies. I threw out the junk food I had and replaced it with healthy food, so I wouldn't be tempted to snack on the bad stuff. The true challenge, however, were all the fast food eateries on my block. Italian, Mexican and Chinese food were literally within a few feet of my doorstep. I wasn't into cooking, so I usually ate out at least four times a week. Fortunately, all of these places had healthy selections on their menus too like grilled veggies or grilled chicken.

However, I had to put my favorite eatery, Pinky's, on notice: "I'm trying to eat healthy, so don't let me order any of my usuals," I told the waitress. In the past, I would have tried to resist on my own, but therapy taught me to ask for help when I needed it. That advice worked perfectly in this instance! The waitress suggested I try out low-calorie versions of my favorite meals, such as having them cooked in Pam or using egg whites with my breakfast instead of the whole egg. Her suggestions helped me big time, because I did not feel like I was depriving myself, and I learned the importance of asking for what I needed.

To be real, there are times when I have an unhealthy craving and I do give in. In the past, I would have worried myself all night with guilt afterwards. Not anymore. Part of "creating a new normal" meant that I had to practice self-forgiveness. It's not the end of the world, I'd remind myself. Tomorrow is a new day. That mantra may sound clichéd, but recovery from trauma, such as I experienced, meant consciously making positive decisions each day and moving forward.

Practicing self-forgiveness enabled me to be more forgiving to others, even those I did not know.

For instance, I would have a bad attitude all day if someone I said "Hi" to did not greet me back. It didn't matter whether or not I knew the person. I would take their lack of response so personally that I would get an ugly attitude with everyone I encountered throughout the rest of the day. As I began to heal, I gained more clarity. Being so self-absorbed in my own problems, it became easy to forget that others had their own personal demons too. Perhaps they were sexually abused, or like me, someone close to them had just died.

I thought about the many people who came into my life and stuck by me despite my negative and often unpredictable behavior. Being forgiving and patient with others was the least I could do, considering so much had been done for me by others. My heart would have been closed to this way of thinking in the past, but "creating this new normal" had opened my heart where once it had been closed. I made a conscious decision to stop taking so many things so personally.

****

It was not easy. Grieving had become a way of life for me. In an odd way, it gave me comfort and assured me that I was keeping my connection and love for Maurice alive. As I engaged in new activities, however, I found the past could no longer hold me back. The sadness slowly began to lift.

The exercise naturally enhanced my mood by increasing the endorphins (happy hormones) in my brain. To keep myself motivated, I started keeping a "good deeds" journal. In this journal I committed to jotting down five good deeds during the course of each day. This task forced me to act with positive purpose each day, thus re-conditioning my long-embedded victim mentality and focusing on the positive in me. Journaling my distractions, however, taught me that I was an emotional eater. I ate when I was sad, lonely or happy. However, I ate the most while mindlessly watching TV. While "creating this new normal," I had an epiphany: I had dedicated so much time to watching actors and actresses live out their dreams on TV, why couldn't I do the same in my own life? Was I not worthy of dedicating just as much if not more time to living out my own dreams instead of being a voyeur into the lives of others? That realization was a life-altering wake-up call. Since then, I've become an avid reader and been able to dedicate a lot more time to my other passion: writing. Socially, I've been getting out to reconnect with friends again. Although, I still watch soap operas, I'm not a slave to them. I no longer plan my day around the soaps. I'll watch only if I happen to be at home.

****

Within two months, I had made significant changes. I lost 15 pounds and cut down on watching television from more than 40 hours a week to less than 5 hours. In the past, these changes would have been temporary, but, as I continued to heal from the emotional damage of my past, it became easier to resist going back to old ways. My different lifestyle was now a new type of normal for me. I no longer desired what was not good for me.

Yes, healing gave me clarity where there was none. I began thinking about my career and what truly brought me passion. What would I do naturally, even if I didn't get paid for it? The answer came instantly — working with sexual abuse survivors. Working on myself let me rediscover my passion for working with sexual abuse survivors. Though still unemployed, I was determined more than ever to help this population, so I resumed teaching my workshop for African-American sexual abuse survivors.

From there I was able to obtain a grant to start an online support group for black sexual abuse survivors, where we help each other heal. It is on a fast track to be one of the largest support groups for African-American sexual abuse survivors! Doing this project has worked wonders for my healing and empowered me in ways no paycheck ever could. Miraculously, each time I share my story with others, the shame lessens and my support system grows broader and stronger. Never in my wildest dreams did I think such joy could come from so much pain. Telling my story is not an option now; it is an obligation. It's an obligation to those who are still in pain, and most importantly, an obligation and prayer of thanks to God. God has blessed me with people along the way, who have helped me overcome many tough obstacles. I must in turn allow Him to use me to help others. Who am I to block someone else's blessing?

However, I had to find a balance between tending to the needs of others and taking care of my own needs. To do so, I asked others to assist with developing the online support group and rearranged my schedule so I could have Sunday's off to take care of me. And I now understand the lessons I learned from my relationship with Maurice: 1) Not everyone can have a front-row seat in your life. Some people you have to love from a distance; 2) Never enable an alcoholic; 3) Tell everyone you love, that you love them while they are here. Despite the fact that I have not yet developed a new romantic relationship, life is fuller than ever. I am still a work in progress, but I am developing a new relationship with myself and, more importantly, I am building a new relationship with God. Evidently, creating a new normal is exactly what I needed to find authentic happiness.